Bill Johnson's new book, *Born for Significance*, is an amazing book that brings balance to much-needed subjects—favor with God and man, reigning in life, promotion, and blessing. Bill takes us down the narrow path, the biblical path, avoiding the view that to be spiritual, we are to be poor, and avoiding the view that not to be rich indicates something is wrong with our faith. In a time when there is so much criticism of the *health and wealth* message, it is refreshing to see someone reveal to us the biblical way to navigate between what I believe are extreme and non-biblical views on both sides. I loved the book, found it fascinating, liberating, enlightening, and encouraging. It was not overly simplistic, nor was it filled with religious platitudes. It was full of the wisdom of God. Bill helps us understand the why of our blessing and favor and how it is meant for us to be a source of blessing to others; we reign in life to serve others. This is a book full of wisdom, one that I can tell has been percolating in Bill for years. In the fullness of time Bill is sharing with us the revelational truths he has ascertained by the Holy Spirit. It is not only a book of wisdom; it is also a book of hope. Bill explains the bedrock basis for such hope in the wisdom of God. This is the kind of book that is so practical you will want to buy others to give to your friends and family.

—Randy Clark
Overseer, The Apostolic Network
of Global Awakening;
President, Global Awakening
Theological Seminary

Bill Johnson is so very dear to my heart. There are few people whom I admire more. His integrity and authenticity are of the highest caliber. I have watched him love his wife, children, grandchildren, and friends, and God's people in a way that is once in a generation. Words cannot express how thankful I am for the measure of Jesus that

Bill Johnson carries. The way he has loved me, my wife, Jessica, and my entire family has changed us forever. I believe this book will carry an anointing that will impact you and the generations to come.

—Michael Koulianos
Evangelist and Founder, Jesus Image

In these conflicted and conflicting times there is not a better book for you to read than *Born for Significance*. Bill Johnson has penned the book for this new era that we are in. You are a child of God who must know your journey and see your path new and fresh. This book is about humility on your walk ahead, promotion on your walk ahead, and perception on your walk ahead. *Born for Significance* is about apprehending favor and walking in victorious, overcoming life in the midst of warfare and rest. As you begin this reading, you are at a certain point on your path of life and path of deliverance. Drink in the words, and learn from one who has been conflicted and yet overcome. Bill Johnson has truly stood the test of an elder in the body of Christ. Receive every word of wisdom he shares within these covers.

—Dr. Chuck D. Pierce
President, Global Spheres;
President, Glory of Zion
International Ministries

Where we live and minister in northern Mozambique, we always say that we want to go lower still—we want to pursue a humble place before God, the place of a servant. It is our honor to do this because we know that everything we lay down, we lay down for the joy set before us—great blessings and eternal life for God's people and His glory revealed on earth. Bill Johnson and his church family have been a tremendous strength and gift to us for many years, through thick and thin. When he writes about becoming a blessing for the sake of those around us, he speaks from experience. We are beyond grateful to call him friend, and pray that you find in his words a fresh hunger for true humility so that you may also carry the full grace and abundance of your calling.

—Heidi G. Baker, PhD
Cofounder and Executive Chairman of the Board, Iris Global

Bill Johnson's new book, *Born for Significance*, took me to school and built my faith both personally and for my family and friends. There have been a handful of books in my life that have been an injection of perspective right on time, and I felt like reading this was one of them. Bill is a master communicator, but even more he speaks out of deep connection to God's heart and demystifies processes that normally feel unattainable. I think this is a key book in the days we are living in to help retire old ways of thinking and upgrade your personal perspective. It will be one of God's kingdom building blocks that will build your maturity so that your heart can be an on-ramp for the promotion and significance that God desires for you!

—Shawn Bolz
TV and Podcast Host, *Exploring the Prophetic*;
Author, *Translating God* and *Breakthrough: Prophecies, Prayers, and Declarations*

Very few men are able to communicate Holy Spirit revelation like Bill Johnson. His writing, like his preaching, is always rich, but this book, *Born for Significance*, might be his best yet. It is a masterpiece—a gift to the body of Christ and I believe it will change your perspective in life altering ways. You only have one life. Make it count!

—Daniel Kolenda
Evangelist;
President and CEO, Christ for All Nations

I believe that we are entering a season where the children of God will have an unprecedented opportunity to reveal their Father's glory in every area and level of society. For God's children to shine this brightly, it is essential that they understand how growth, promotion, and identity work within God's kingdom, and I have never read a more insightful and empowering guide to this process than Bill Johnson's *Born for Significance*. It is an invitation to a lifelong journey of sustained glory and a potentially lifesaving guide to the pitfalls that would undermine that journey.

—Blake Healy
Author, *The Veil*;
Director, Bethel Atlanta School of
Supernatural Ministry

# BORN FOR SIGNIFICANCE

BILL JOHNSON

Most Charisma House Book Group products are available at special quantity discounts for bulk purchase for sales promotions, premiums, fund-raising, and educational needs. For details, call us at (407) 333-0600 or visit our website at www.charismahouse.com.

Born for Significance by Bill Johnson
Published by Charisma House
Charisma Media/Charisma House Book Group
600 Rinehart Road, Lake Mary, Florida 32746



All italics in Scripture quotations represent the author's emphasis.



Visit the author's website at bjm.org.

Library of Congress Cataloging-in-Publication Data:
An application to register this book for cataloging has been submitted to the Library of Congress.
International Standard Book Number: 978-1-62999-838-1
E-book ISBN: 978-1-62999-839-8



20 21 22 23 24 — 987654321
Printed in the United States of America

I'd like to dedicate this book to Shawn and Cherie Bolz. They have been personal friends for many years. In fact, I had the privilege of performing their wedding. During our many years of friendship, co-laboring together in ministry, I have watched them continually fight for and protect the significance of each person. It didn't matter how rich or poor that person was, or how secular or religious the person's role may have been in society. I love them and their approach to life. They bring great freedom to all who receive from them.

To Shawn and Cherie: You have inspired me greatly. Thanks for helping to recalibrate the purpose of the prophetic in this day and age. I love you both.

I had this thought a couple of years ago that has both inspired and protected the uniqueness of the individual: *If you knew who God made you to be, you'd never want to be anyone else.* Shawn and Cherie model this well, empowering people to become all that God intended—*born for significance*!

# CONTENTS

# ACKNOWLEDGMENTS

I WANT TO THANK my personal staff for their help in all I do: Michael Van Tinteren, Kelsey King, and Abigail McKoy. Special thanks go to Pam Spinosi, whose input and editing helped make this book possible. I also want to thank my friend Stephen Strang and Charisma Media for taking on this project, with special thanks to Debbie Marrie for her editing help and patience. Thanks to all of them for their labor of love.

# FOREWORD

Unless it's been suppressed, each one of us has an innate desire for *significance* and *success*. These two desires are closely related, as we long to live a life that matters. But in order to do so, we must first realize that our significance comes from *who we are* (identity), and success is a result of *what we do* (purpose).

Many have stumbled when they attempt to find significance from *what they do* rather than from *who they are*. This in turn produces a performance-based identity, which will always leave you searching and striving to do more so you can become more.

Here's what I'm saying: each believer is saved by grace to first *be someone—a child of God, and we are equally empowered by that same grace to do something*. (See Ephesians 2:8–10.) These two truths are inseparable. We can never overemphasize one truth to the neglect of another truth. Significance, therefore, is realized by the outworking of both identity and purpose. I cannot emphasize enough that *who we are* in Christ Jesus is paramount to *what we do*—for anything we do should be an outflow of who we are.

Here's another reason we often get things twisted: we forget that God is eternal. He therefore does not view our lives the same way we often do. For this reason, God's definitions of *significance* and *success* are not our earthly, human definitions. According to the world's standard, many believers throughout history who were martyred for their faith would be considered failures. Not so to God—He sees things through the lens of eternity!

In Psalm 90:17 Moses asked God (not once but twice) to "make our efforts successful." First, Hebrew writers didn't waste words. They didn't repeat things just to fill in extra space. In fact, when they did repeat something, it was to intentionally bring emphasis, much in the same way we might write something in bold, italics, or all capital letters. Second, those words come from Scripture, revealing to us God's intent for our lives. Yes, God's desire is to help us be successful! Yet we must remember that God has a much different perspective toward significance and success than we do.

Our world is continually changing. Names are remembered for a time, and legacies endure for a season, but history eventually moves on. Even the things we consider to be most certain now will vastly transform or cease to exist only a few hundred years from now.

It is not so with God. He never changes. From the beginning to the end, throughout all eternity, God will remain the same. His standard will never change. His heart toward us will never change. His definitions of *significance* and *success* will never change.

If we are to truly succeed in life, then we must succeed by God's eternal definition. All other success will one day fail. Only success by God's standard will endure. I'm thrilled that my dear friend Bill Johnson has written *Born for Significance*. I have high respect for Bill. His life is an open book that invites us all to actively partake in the outworking of God's story upon the earth—a story that bridges the realities of heaven to the needs of mankind. If you want to awaken to a life of significance, then the words that follow will supply the fuel you need to make your life count, both now and for eternity.

This book is more than just words on paper; its message is the outflow of a life well lived. Regardless of your race, gender, or vocation, you were born for significance!

—John Bevere
Best-Selling Author and Minister
Cofounder, Messenger International

# INTRODUCTION

THIS BOOK IS *not* an invitation to wealth, fame, or power *in Jesus' name.* It is an invitation to a lifetime journey, in the fear of the Lord, to discover all that God intended us to become in this life.

Our greatest challenges often have to do with learning to walk in humility while experiencing ever-increasing significance and influence. In reaction, many believers have chosen insignificance simply because it's easier to manage a life from which little is expected. Tragically the church usually calls this *humility.* It is not. Denying God's purpose for our lives is anything but humility. For this reason, fear is often called *wisdom* by those bound by it. It's time to shed these restrictions that have masqueraded as virtues and say yes to God's invitation to significance.

But our significance must be according to His definition. "Become as a child." "Become the servant of all." These are the things that we all say amen to in principle. But we rarely address what follows these decisions to become poor in spirit: promotion. When we say yes to becoming little in our own eyes, willing to be the servant to everyone around us, God has found someone He can trust with societal promotion.

Now what? Read on, and together let's discover His wonderful intention for the church, His body, the literal dwelling place of the Holy Spirit on earth.

# PART I

# THE PURPOSE OF PROMOTION

## CHAPTER 1

# WELCOME TO THE CONFLICTED LIFE

It is no secret that this glorious walk with Jesus is one of conflict, challenge, and, of course, extreme blessing. The conflict, however, is often within. In other words, it's not only the external part of a life of hard circumstances or struggles with people. Much of the conflict is on the inside as we try to learn how this life in Christ is supposed to work. Our way of thinking is quite different from what we find on the pages of Scripture, which reveals the mind of Christ. God's way of thinking is completely different from ours, and He isn't going to change. Not only does He often contradict what and how we think; He sometimes seems to be in conflict with Himself. That is a foolish conclusion, I know, and comes from human reasoning only. But it reveals at least part of the reason for our internal struggles in this conflicted life, as you can only live where you've died.

---

The main point we should be learning in this quandary is simple yet profound. The Word of God is best understood *in relationship with God. #bornforsignificance*

---

The Bible is filled with these examples, of which I will mention a few to give context. We find one great illustration of this conflict in Proverbs 26:4–5. He says, "Do not answer a fool according to his folly, lest you also be like him. Answer a fool according to his folly, lest he be wise in his own eyes" (NKJV). There they are, back-to-back verses commanding us to do opposite things. Don't speak to the fool. Speak to the fool.

We find similar cases throughout Scripture. Here's an example in the life of the apostle Paul. Jesus commanded His followers to go into the whole world and preach the gospel. And yet when Paul tried to go to Asia to carry out this commission, which is obviously part of the *whole world*, the Holy Spirit said no. He was then directed in a dream to go to Macedonia. He openly obeyed a command, only to be told no, and was then redirected.

---

The Bible is so much more than a book of principles that I can mimic to be successful. It is by nature an invitation to walk with the author. *#bornforsignificance*

---

Another example is where Jesus instructed us to love our neighbors as we love ourselves. Self-love then seems to be a necessary part of effectively loving our neighbors. And yet in his letter to Timothy, Paul warned against those who in the last days would be lovers of self. So do we love ourselves or not? These are not really contradictions, but they do remind us of our need to stay close to His heart to know what to do in a given situation.

## JESUS, THE TEACHER

Jesus' teaching often created these challenges. He taught us that in order to live, we would have to die. He required His followers to go last in order to be first, give to receive, and humble themselves to be exalted. He also taught that those who mourn would find joy and comfort, and the persecuted would be happy. (The word *blessed* means happy.) The list goes on and on. The main point we should be learning in this quandary is simple yet profound. The Word of God is best understood *in relationship with God.* The Bible is so much more than a book of principles that I can mimic to be successful. It is by nature an invitation to walk with the author. This is the only way I can know whether to answer the fool.

When it comes to how we should live, there is only so much we can extract from God's Word without the Holy Spirit making it clear in the context of our connection with Him. And it is the Holy Spirit who enables us to do what we read. We can certainly learn about kindness, generosity, courage, and the like as we, through human reasoning, try to extract the principles for life from the pages of Scripture. But the power for personal transformation is found in a relationship with the One who is both the author and revealer of truth. My need for His input is more than daily. It is moment by moment. He lives in me, in part, for that reason.

## WHAT ABOUT SIGNIFICANCE?

It can be said we must first discover our insignificance to discover our significance, knowing there is nothing we can do to save ourselves or improve our lives in light of eternity apart from God. We can't get to heaven on our own. This puts us in a place of complete abandonment and trust, which is quite humbling. We can make decisions to improve our lives, but we can't change our nature in any substantial way. We are marked by sin itself and need help from the outside to become free.

Many people work hard at developing proper self-esteem. The need is real and great. But since we were made in the image of God, our true self-worth comes from our understanding of Him and His nature. Seeing Him more clearly is what positions us to see ourselves from His point of view more clearly.

God did not create us because He needed us. That would make Him, who is eternal, incomplete for all of eternity past. God is without need and self-contained. He did not create us to satisfy His need; He has none. Instead, we were made from His dream, His desire. In light of that it can be said that the value, or *significance*, of something is determined by what someone is willing to pay. Considering that the Father gave His Son, and Jesus gave His life, and the Holy Spirit lives in imperfect vessels, there is reason to believe our value is far beyond our ability to comprehend. God Himself then underscores our significance quite heavily. Only in a relationship with Him do we find the singular pathway for this discovery.

## NICE TRY

Many who have caught glimpses of the victorious Christian life have, through the *arm of flesh*, built up their self-confidence, which is a poor copy of faith and triumph. Self-confidence is no greater than self. Real faith is as great as God and has its foundation in His nature and person. Such confidence in God then is superior to every other expression in life because it is founded in the person of God Himself. It is not built through striving. It comes entirely through surrender. It dwells in real humility, which is a far cry from self-criticism and condemnation. Real faith moves mountains and is the yielded partnership with His nature. I find significance and confidence when I discover that as a born-again believer, I am in Christ. Therein lies my significance. As a result, my significance is more substantial than I ever could have wished for myself before my surrender to this perfect Father.

---

Self-confidence is no greater than self. Real faith is as great as God and has its foundation in His nature and person. *#bornforsignificance*

---

We must admit that we see through a glass darkly, groping to find what has eluded us for generations: a clear understanding of the victory provided for us through the cross and resurrection that is to affect every area of life! Yes, of course, this must be seen in our victory over sin. But what about victory as it pertains to family life? Or maybe the way it is to be seen in our physical health, or even the taboo subject of finances? What about our mental and emotional health? What about the God dreams connected with the call and purpose for our lives? And then there are the places of service to which God has called us outside of pulpit ministry and the wonderful area of traditional world missions. What does it look like for the believer to illustrate the resurrection power of Jesus in every part of life in our communities, including the marketplace? Is that even possible? Perhaps we should ask if it is even desirable.

I believe it is not only desirable but also *required* of this generation to pursue what has been out of view for centuries, that by God's grace this has been moved to the forefront in our pursuit of *reformation*, *awakening*, and *renaissance*. These three terms, often used interchangeably, describe different aspects of what is available to those who pursue their place of responsibility of the gospel in this hour. I love these themes, as they give purpose to the significance of our role in society. My job is not to go to heaven; it is to bring heaven down, in whatever measure His will allows. This is accomplished through prayer and obedience.

## OUR CHALLENGE

The question I then must ask is this: Is it possible to bear my cross and step into a place of resurrection life that illustrates a life of freedom in God? The term I will use throughout this book is *reigning in life.* Reigning in life is succeeding in a way that glorifies God through the realized effect of the death and resurrection of Christ. This concept is the key to understanding the Book of Proverbs, as all wisdom is given to equip us for reigning in life. Paul also addresses this subject in His discourse on our salvation in Romans 5:17: "Those who receive the abundance of grace and of the gift of righteousness will *reign in life* through the One, Jesus Christ." This is an essential aspect of our lives in Christ. It illustrates the effect of His righteousness and grace on our broken but surrendered lives.

---

My job is not to go to heaven; it is to bring heaven down, in whatever measure His will allows. *#bornforsignificance*

---

So I ask again, What is blessing supposed to look like in the practical parts of life? Can it be measured in our personal lives, our finances, our health, our positions of influence, and so on? Is *reigning in life* supposed to play a role in the Great Commission? This seems to be a primary lesson in Psalm 67. It is a prayer for personal blessing, a favor, "that your way would be known on earth, and your salvation to the nations." There it is: the Great Commission—salvation for nations.

My frustration is in the constant run-in with those who have greater faith in the return of Jesus than they do in the power of the gospel. His return will be great and glorious and is to be desired. But His return fixes nothing for the world, which is supposed to be our assignment and priority. It only serves us. We must regain our confidence in the power of the good news to transform a life, a family, a neighborhood, a city, a state, and a nation. If it can bring transformation to one of these elements in life, it can do it for all. And it must.

## THE CHALLENGE OF EXTREMES

On the one hand, we have those who believe that lack or poverty is the mark of spirituality. To them Jesus had no place to lay His head and owned nothing but the clothes on His back, so if we own nothing, it is supposed to represent that we are genuine disciples. This logic breaks down quite easily in that it wasn't taught in the writings of the apostles in the epistles. Neither was it practiced by the first-generation church, who had the most direct influence from Jesus and the apostles. This idea is based on one aspect of Jesus' teaching without considering the rest. And quite strangely, those who live this way feed quite happily from the contributions of those with resources. This is hypocritical, the way I see it. If the process for creating wealth is evil, then it also has to be evil to benefit from those resources by receiving offerings.

What I find interesting is that most of the harshest critics of prosperity in the life of a believer criticize because of the one side of Jesus' teaching to sell all and follow Him. This rationale against the idea of a believer being blessed is used by people who have rarely sold all to follow Him, making their argument a moot point.

On the other hand, often in reaction to that way of thinking, we find those who teach that we measure spirituality by our possessions, income, and status on the world stage. We can't find that in Jesus' teaching or example either. It is quite contrary to the life Jesus led. Neither was it taught or practiced by the early church fathers. So forgive my bluntness, but I consider both teachings to be reactions to each other, sick representations of the King and His kingdom. These issues must be settled if we're ever going to be successful in the command to disciple nations.

We are designed to reign in life through prosperity of soul. Our inner world defines our outer world. Only in the context of great favor and promotion can we succeed at making disciples of nations. Even Jesus grew in favor with God and man. It's time we recognize the need for favor in both realms in order to succeed at our assignment.

## TO RULE OR TO SERVE

Many know of the command to love and serve people. But did you know that we are also commanded to rule? All government has these two basic responsibilities before God: to rule and to serve. Our assignment to rule is for protecting. Our assignment to serve is for empowering. In other words, we rule to protect, and we serve to empower.

It doesn't matter if we're talking about the president of a nation, the CEO of a corporation, or the mom and dad of a home. We rule to protect. Ruling is not for self-promotion or self-benefit. Authority is given to us in differing measures to speak on behalf of those who have little to no voice, bringing divine justice and safety through the faithful stewardship of our influence.

God warned Israel of their desire for a king because those individuals would eventually turn their role into one of self-service. The greater the authority that rests upon a person, the greater that person's ability to bring change and transformation. Tragically, authority can also bring destruction if misused.

---

We must learn to rule with the heart of a servant and serve with the heart of a king. It may take us a lifetime to learn this well, but it is a worthwhile journey. *#bornforsignificance*

---

These same principles are true for the church and family. When Paul addresses elders in the church, he states, "The elders who *rule well* are to be considered worthy of double honor" (1 Tim. 5:17). Elders rule the church. Parents are to rule their households well.

Jesus modeled both ruling and serving. He is both the King of all kings and the servant of all. His perspective is what makes the discovery of our significance a safe journey in that each role has its purpose of glorifying Him in everything. The bottom line is that we must learn to *rule with the heart of a servant and serve with the heart of a king*. It may take us a lifetime to learn this well, but it is a worthwhile journey.

## THE PURPOSE OF BLESSING

On many occasions, I've told our church family that if they don't want more, they're selfish. Of everything I've ever said, that statement is one of the easiest to criticize. And while I can make a strong biblical case against it, I also believe it is entirely accurate in the context in which I speak it.

Of course, many automatically think I'm saying we should want wealth, fame, and power. These things are poor counterfeits of kingdom influence and authority. They are the wrong focus entirely. And while it is true that God releases these things into people's lives in different measures and fascinating ways, my approach to this subject is quite different.

We are all surrounded by the needs of people—economic, emotional, physical, relational, mental, and spiritual. The list is endless. To be specific, some not only need a meal; they also need a job restored so they can become a contributor to society and recover the dignity lost through their time of trial, their bout with injustice, or even their season of living with the fruit of poor choices.

The weaker I am in the economic picture, the less I can do to meet some of these needs. And while no one person can fix the problem on a global scale, I want to be able to do more than I can right now. For this reason, I must ache for more resources, favor, and wisdom. But it must be the kind of increase that grows through righteous stewardship. It is my responsibility to make this known to Him in my private times of prayer. The issue of injustice is often the cause of poverty. "Abundant food is in the fallow ground of the poor, but it is swept away by injustice" (Prov. 13:23). Money doesn't fix the problem of poverty. But poverty also can't be fixed without money. Only those who rightly use their God-given authority can solve the issues of injustice.

Sometimes I'm overwhelmed by the deep cries of broken people. Their emotional needs are so extreme that they could unintentionally drain the average believer beyond reason. These broken ones need to lean on the strength of others until they find their bearings again.

Of course, it is God who heals and restores, but He uses people. In 3 John 2, we find there is a *prosperity of soul* available to all of us. We are designed with the potential to be wealthy on the inside. What would it look like if my inner world, my soul, were as prosperous as the richest man in the natural world? Why should we expect less from God for our internal prosperity than the financial condition of the wealthiest of the wealthy? Since the Holy Spirit is the source of unlimited internal wealth of heart and mind, our potential is limitless. And while that potential is in the life of every believer, there's a vast difference between what's in our account (in Christ) and what's in our possession (our daily lifestyle.)

When Peter ministered healing to the man at the Beautiful Gate (Acts 3:8), the account records this lame man "walked, leaped, and praised God." He walked because He was physically healed. He leaped because he was emotionally healed. And he praised God because he was spiritually healed. Peter gave what he had, and it was enough for the complete restoration of this very broken man.

I've had many occasions when demons have left people's bodies when I've prayed for them. It is a unique joy to see such liberty come on the countenance of these dear ones. But I've also had times when very tormented people left in the same condition in which they came. And while I can think of a number of valid reasons that the person left in bondage, the answers don't satisfy me. We have no record in the Gospels of it happening that way for Jesus, and He is our greatest example.

There were extreme cases of demon possession recorded in the Bible, such as the man of the Gadarenes. He was delivered in a moment. It was Jesus' one-step program—out of darkness into His marvelous light. I believe a greater anointing on my life would have helped so many who were not helped. Perhaps this is why Paul said we were to "desire earnestly spiritual gifts" (1 Cor. 14:1). There must be a cry in me for "the more" of God to rest upon my life, as the need around me is not getting smaller; it's increasing dramatically. And so is the compassion in me for their breakthroughs.

While examples of our need for more could fill this entire book, I hope you get the point. We must hunger in the secret place with God for the more He has made available so that we might be the blessing we were designed to be—all for the sake of others.

## THE REST OF THE STORY

Let me start by addressing what I view as our greatest challenge. Without the cross, we have nothing in this life of following Jesus. Denying ourselves for the sake of Christ is the only reasonable way to live. Yet the life of a believer is the life of resurrection. The cross must lead us to something, and this something is the place of triumph. Victory over sin, torment, disease, and the like is a manifestation of the resurrection power of Jesus.

---

Reaction gives me a conclusion; response connects me to a process. *#bornforsignificance*

---

Jesus didn't stay on the cross, nor did He stay in the grave. He rose from the dead to give us new life. What does that life look like when the blessing of His resurrection touches our health, our finances, or our place in society?

To be honest, it's easy to live in *reaction* to whatever error offends me the most (either poverty or wealth as signs of spirituality). It's much more challenging to live in *response* to what the Father is saying and doing in these areas. Reaction gives me a conclusion; response connects me to a process. And this process takes me somewhere, which is beyond all we have the intelligence or faith to ask for ourselves. Herein lies one of the greatest mysteries of the Christian life, found in 1 John 4:17: "As He is, so also are we in this world." This was written by the apostle John, the one who was with Jesus before His death at the last supper, who had his head on Jesus' chest. This same John then saw Jesus some time later in His glorified state in Revelation chapter 1. It was this John who wrote, "As He is..." Our life is patterned after the One who is raised from the dead, ascended to the right hand of the Father, and forever glorified. It almost sounds blasphemous to say, but our walk with Jesus is not patterned after His pre-glorified state. It is firmly established in the victorious Christ! Jesus taught us the ways of the kingdom in His earthly life. His humility, boldness, passion, and love are all eternal. These traits never change, whether it's before the cross or after. This is who the Son of God has always been, always will be. They remain true, no matter the season of our lives. But His resurrection, ascension, and glorification are to change much of what we expect of our lives in that we live from the absolute victory of Christ.

The Christian life is one of conflict between the issue of blessing and the issue of the cross. There's probably no greater area of disagreement in the church than when it comes to money. And while I don't intend to make this book or even this chapter about money, it's a natural standard to use, as it is the easiest to measure.

Most believers can quote Jesus' command to the rich young ruler to sell everything he had and give to the poor. Jesus knew what occupied the center of this young man's heart. It was vital for him to make the exchange from Lord Mammon to Lord Jesus. But he was unwilling.

Tragically, few live with an awareness of the other half of that vital bit of instruction. Once again, we find ourselves in the conflicted life.

Here's a great passage on this subject from Mark 10:23–25, 28–31:

> And Jesus, looking around, said to His disciples, "How hard it will be for those who are wealthy to enter the kingdom of God!" The disciples were amazed at His words. But Jesus answered again and said to them, "Children, how hard it is to enter the kingdom of God! It is easier for a camel to go through the eye of a needle than for a rich man to enter the kingdom of God."
>
> Peter began to say to Him, "Behold, we have left everything and followed You." Jesus said, "Truly I say to you, there is no one who has left house or brothers or sisters or mother or father or children or farms, for My sake and for the gospel's sake, but that *he will receive a hundred times as much* now in the present age, houses and brothers and sisters and mothers and children and farms, along with persecutions; and in the age to come, eternal life. But many who are first will be last, and the last, first."

In this chapter, Jesus deals swiftly with the threat of wealth on a believer's life. When Peter reminds Jesus that they left everything to follow Him, He surprises them with His answer: "He will receive a hundred times as much now in the present age, houses and brothers and sisters and mothers and children and farms, along with persecutions; and in the age to come, eternal life." We know Jesus isn't talking about our being blessed in eternity, as there is no persecution there. Forgive my brashness, but it appears that Jesus points to money/wealth/blessing saying *it will kill you.* And then He says He will pour one hundred times as much of what *will kill you* back into their lives. I'm sure this is an overstatement, but I hope you get my point. It is the cross (leaving all) that gives them access to the resurrection (a hundredfold return on what they left).

His answer to Peter is rarely quoted and not nearly as often as the first half of the dialogue. I'm sure the reason for this is the fact that we don't want any more self-serving Christians who wish to follow Jesus for personal gain and profit. But it is my conviction that if we don't learn how to manage blessings correctly, we'll never enter the place He intended for us in bringing true reformation, awakening, and renaissance to our nations. This is the rest of the story. All of this is for the purpose of fulfilling the commission Jesus gave us to disciple nations.

## PAUL SPEAKS

There's no one who better illustrates what it is to follow Jesus to me than the apostle Paul. His life of abandonment to Jesus is convicting and inspiring at the same time. His insights and instruction for the church are flawless. Here he speaks to the wealthy through 1 Timothy 6:17–19:

> Instruct those who are rich in this present world not to be conceited or to fix their hope on the uncertainty of riches, but on God, who richly supplies us with all things to enjoy. Instruct them to do good, to be rich in good works, to be generous and ready to share, storing up for themselves the treasure of a good foundation for the future, so that they may take hold of that which is life indeed.

Let's unpack some principles from this scripture that we can apply to any manifestation of blessing, whether it be health, position, legacy, or others.

**1. Don't let blessings make you conceited.**

This implies that wealth of any kind can make people proud and independent, thinking that they earned or deserved the blessing. Blessings create entitlement without humility and thankfulness. One of my favorite verses is "The horse is prepared for the day of battle, but the victory belongs to the Lord" (Prov. 21:31). I love this verse because it reveals how the natural and supernatural realms are to merge. On the one hand, there is our effort, discipline, and training. But even then, God gets all the credit for everything we worked so hard at. He enabled us and gave us strength, wisdom, and opportunity. Removing Him from the equation is the most dangerous expression of foolishness, leading certainly to destructive pride. I must do all I can do to ensure victory, so to speak, but at the end of the day, I must live with the realization that the victory only came through the grace of God. Any other way of thinking will become the fly in the ointment that I will suffer for in the end.

**2. Don't fix hope on the uncertainty of riches.**

I often ask people how much money is too much money. As I write this, governments and institutions are trying to solve that puzzle right now through high taxes and other forms of punishment. But I believe it comes down to this: too much is whatever amount replaces trust. For one person, it is $1,000 in the bank. For another, it is $100,000,000. It's not an amount. It's how the blessing affects our relational trust in Jesus. Money, or blessing in general, is not stable enough to carry the weight of faith. Only Jesus is perfectly faithful and worthy of undefiled trust.

**3. God richly supplies us with all things to enjoy.**

Blessings are to endear us to Him with delight and joy. His supply is abundant, and it must lead us to the legitimate kingdom expression of pleasure. It is to be enjoyed. When increase causes us to become separate from human need and independent from our divine purpose, we falter.

**4. Do good, be rich in good works, and be generous and ready to share.**

In the end, the blessings of the Lord—whether they be finances, favor, position, or insights—are to be used for the benefit of others. Good works, generosity, and a lifestyle of fellowship with other believers are to be the hallmarks of the blessed life. Blessings position us to affect another person's life for the better. Generosity—whether through financing, serving, or granting opportunity—produces thankfulness in the heart of the one who receives, which brings glory to God. And that is the goal of all things: for God to be glorified.

## THE OLD COVENANT SPEAKS

One of the fundamental conflicts we have in the whole of Scripture is not so much between law and grace, but the promises, blessings, and lifestyles of the Old Testament saint versus those of us in the New Testament. What do the blessings of God look like in the Old versus the New? Clearly, they were natural before the cross, and they are primarily spiritual and eternal once one has been born again. But do the natural blessings and promises of the Old Testament still apply to New Testament believers?

It will help us if we can learn to recognize what ended at the cross, what changed at the cross, and what came through the cross unchanged. I believe that ignoring this issue will cost us dearly, as God has left precious treasures for the New Testament believer in the whole Bible. Romans 15:4 says, "For whatever was written in earlier times *was written for our instruction*, so that through perseverance and the encouragement of the Scriptures we might have hope." The Old Testament was written for the New Testament believer as much as it was for those in the day it was written. From this passage we see that hope is the fruit of embracing the whole of Scripture. The following illustrates our challenge.

1. **What ended at the cross:** Animal sacrifices ended at the cross. Jesus died once and for all, putting an end to the need of shedding blood for the temporary postponement of sin's penalty.
2. **What was changed at the cross:** When Jesus announced the favorable year of the Lord, He announced every year to be the year of Jubilee. Under the Old Covenant, the year of Jubilee took place every fifty years. This was when all debts were canceled, slaves were set free, and property boundaries were reestablished to the original borders. Because of the cross, Jesus was able to announce that Jubilee is no longer just every fifty years. It is now.
3. **What made it through the cross unchanged:** Worship today is basically the same as it was in David's day. He instituted something new and unusual: musical instruments, singing, choirs, dancing, and other physical expressions were all given as offerings to Him, the audience of One. Our great privilege in life is to minister to God,

> which David explored in ways not known before. These were all new expressions of thanksgiving, praise, and worship. David's example became the new norm. Amos 9:11–12 declared this would be a last-days reality, just as it was in David's day. This fulfillment was recognized by the apostles in Acts 15:16–18.

Jesus teaches that we are not to make natural wealth our goal. Paul affirms this value in teaching and practice. But then even Solomon, the richest man ever, teaches the same in Proverbs. He stated that we are not to weary ourselves to obtain wealth, for it makes itself wings and flies away.

More specifically, the Old Testament promises wealth and well-being to those who obey God. In fact, the Hebrew word *shalom* contains just about everything we will ever need in life in its definition. It means sound mind, well-being, health, prosperity, and on and on. The point is, these blessings are interwoven throughout the Old Testament as the reward for obeying God.

I read two psalms in prophetic intercessory prayer over my household every day: Psalm 127 and Psalm 128. I especially enjoy them in The Passion Translation. Here's Psalm 128:

> How joyous are those who love the Lord and bow low before God, ready to obey him! Your reward will be prosperity, happiness, and well-being. Your wife will bless your heart and home. Your children will bring you joy as they gather around your table. Yes, this is God's generous reward for those who love him. May the Lord bless you out of his Zion-glory! May you see the prosperity of Jerusalem throughout your lifetime. And may you be surrounded by your grandchildren. Happiness to you! And happiness to Israel!

This psalm declares prosperity, happiness, and well-being as rewards for obeying God in humility. It goes on to say this blessed person will experience multigenerational health in their family and they will eventually influence an entire city by that blessing.

## DAVID'S VALUE FOR REWARDS

We often think of David killing Goliath as a demonstration of his zeal for God. It is, but notice that he was also motivated by a healthy desire for reward.

Israel lined up in battle array but wanted to do anything but fight. A giant of the Philistine army named Goliath wanted to fight someone. There was no one, including King Saul, with the courage to fight him. David's father, Jesse, sent him to the frontlines to bring food to his other sons. David brought the food and stood with the soldiers. When he overheard the reward for killing Goliath, his interests perked up. Whoever slew this giant would get Saul's beautiful daughter as a wife, as well as riches and a lifetime free of taxes for his family.

It's a funny story, especially in light of how many believers won't discuss or allow themselves to want rewards from God. But David asked someone else about the rewards for killing Goliath, again. And then again. Even his brothers were annoyed about this young man being with the men. I'm sure their cowardice was being exposed by the courage of their younger brother.

David became righteously indignant. He told Saul the story of how he had killed the lion and the bear and was now ready to kill this mere man, who taunted the armies of the living God. The righteous jealousy for the Lord was real. And so was his desire for reward. What followed is one of the most well-known stories in the Bible. People who have never read the Bible can tell it in great detail. It has become a cultural proverb for how the underdog defeats their foe. We use it in sports, politics, and the corporate world. But it started with a young man who was jealous for God and at the same time longed for promotion.

For those who think it unspiritual to look for promotion and reward, I remind you of two things:

1. Jesus endured the cross for the joy set before Him. (See Hebrews 12:2.) Joy was the reward for His suffering.
2. Faith believes He is and that He is the One who rewards those who diligently seek Him. (See Hebrews 11:6.)

Reward is an essential part of authentic faith. Without it we don't understand what God called us to when He called us to a life of faith. Jesus talked about rewards quite liberally. We can never think it is humility to ignore what Jesus spoke about.

David became provoked and killed Goliath with a stone. And as they say, the rest is history. It is not healthy to deflect honor in the moments when it is given. When someone compliments you, don't say, "It wasn't me; it was Jesus." If you ever say that to me, I'll likely respond, "Oh, it was good, but not *that* good!" That's my humorous way of pointing out that it's best to receive the compliment. Enjoy the moment of honor and let it encourage you as it was intended to do. Then, when you're alone, give it to the One who deserves it most. "Jesus, here, this was given to me, and it belongs to You. Thank You for the privilege of co-laboring with You." Besides, if we don't know how to receive honor, we'll have no crown to throw at His feet, which is a concept found in Revelation 4:10.

## A PASTOR'S DELIGHT

As a pastor, I strongly emphasize spiritual responsibilities and how they affect eternity. I consider eternity to be the cornerstone of logic and reason for a kingdom-minded person. Once we remove eternity from the equation, we remove design, purpose, and destiny. And once those issues are out of our consciousness, no longer is there awareness or burden for the subject of accountability. This is where we stand before God to give an account of our lives. For this reason, great wisdom comes from living with a consciousness of eternity.

I don't like the emphasis of many that use wealth and fame as a measuring rod to how well someone is doing in their efforts to follow Jesus. And yet I don't know of any pastors who do not rejoice if one of their members becomes the mayor of their city, the CEO of a major corporation, or the star athlete who signs a huge contract with a professional sports team. It's not about their increase in tithe or financial support, either. It really is about the joy of seeing the people we care for come into the fulfillment of their purpose and destiny. It's what we do. We delight in other people's promotions. But sadly, we rarely have the courage to teach this as a possible way that God would bless or cause a person to be successful. I hope to be able to speak to this issue as well as equip the believer to become all that God intended. For anyone who discovers who God made them to be would never want to be anyone else.

## CHAPTER 2

# IDENTITY AND PROMOTION

PROMOTION IS HOW we advance in position, rank, and influence. And while titles don't always reflect our significance in the kingdom of God, they can be measurements by which we see our role to the world around us. But what must be maintained as a value of the kingdom is the only promotion worth pursuing is the one that comes from God. All other promotions are ultimately setbacks in our personal development and potential. Self-promotion undermines the process that God has assigned for each of our lives. Whatever I *obtain* through self-promotion I'll have to *sustain* through self-promotion. It's like a beach ball with a leak. The only way to keep it full is to continue pumping it full of air. It's a lot of work. And it takes away from the purpose of the beach ball, which illustrates the plan and promotion that God had in place for us.

Instead of spending our time and effort on our purpose in life, we pour it out for things that bear no lasting fruit. And there's a day coming when we will each stand before the Lord to give an account for how we lived our lives. On that day the *fruit that remains* is all that will matter to us.

---

Whatever I *obtain* through self-promotion I'll have to *sustain* through self-promotion. *#bornforsignificance*

---

Promotion is in the heart of God for each of us. He is the perfect Father, who delights in our growth and maturity as we learn to represent Him well in all areas of life. We do this by becoming like Jesus in character and then by stewarding the increase of responsibilities as citizens of His kingdom. Proper stewardship of gifts and opportunities in life opens doors for us to step into more significant roles as followers of Jesus.

## TITLES, MONEY, AND POWER

It probably needs to be said at this point that promotion for the believer is not always about title, money, or power. While it may include any number of external things, it really is about being more like Jesus in our inner world. More specifically, this has to do with our thought life, our emotional health, and our overall bent toward the will of God. Representing (read *re*-presenting) Jesus on earth is the goal. From that place of personal victory, we can demonstrate the reality of His presence and kingdom to the world around us, which automatically brings an increase in responsibilities and potential impact.

There's no question that His promotion sometimes includes title, position, power, and resource. But those things make for terrible goals in our journey. *Seeking first the kingdom of God* is the challenge we face. Seeking first the kingdom is basically to pursue the reality of the King's dominion to be released over the broken, diseased, and inferior situations in life. The promise He gave us is that all the other stuff needed to fulfill our purpose would be added to us. Becoming more like Jesus positions us to be effective in bringing lasting change to the world around us.

We become a danger to ourselves when our focus or objective becomes the things that are supposed to be added to our lives as the fruit of our God-given priorities. When that happens, our pursuit of the kingdom becomes a smoke screen for our real ambition of personal gain. Our place of significance is to seek the full expression of the lordship/kingship of Jesus into needful situations we run into throughout our lives. If we choose to seek the reward instead of His rule, we cut short our development and restrict our ability to experience and manifest the reality of His kingdom through our surrendered lives.

To "seek first the kingdom" is the process; "all these things will be added" is the outcome. *We* love outcomes. *He* treasures the process or journey. To grow in this kingdom, we must learn to treasure what He treasures and give attention to the things that have captured His heart. When we become kingdom-minded people and truly make that the priority of our pursuits in life, we place ourselves in the position that He celebrates most. When we get those priorities mixed up, He cuts back our rewards to the measure we can faithfully steward without losing our heart for His kingdom.

## MISTAKEN IDENTITY

It is so easy to draw our identity from inferior things. Possessions, jobs, education, and titles are a small part of this infinite list. But busyness is perhaps the surprise entry and is probably at the top of the list for many. It can make one feel important. But neither identity nor significance should be defined by our schedules.

Busyness is artificial significance. Many believers clutter their lives with Christian activities, thinking that demonstrates their heart for the will of God in their lives. As a result, they tragically never have to learn how to reign in life amid the chaos of the worldly systems that surround us. Schedules often take us out of the necessary interactions with unbelievers that keep us aware of what we do well and what we don't. Busyness also tends to insulate us from the divine reasoning that enables us to rise to our potential in areas that are not overtly spiritual.

Reigning in life is not reigning over people. We are called to reign in life in the sense that we manage the issues of our own lives under the direct leadership of God. (See Romans 5:17.) For example, money doesn't control me. I control money in a way that glorifies God. Relationships don't control me, whether they are good or bad. I manage my relationships God's way that He might receive honor and that I might find healthy community. Reigning in life as citizens of His kingdom gives us a position of favor that makes our service effective.

## THE RESTED LIFESTYLE

Avoiding rest is a violation of our design. Not even God worked seven days, and yet many today praise the hard workers who give themselves to their assignment without rest. Even the church celebrates devoted pastors who pour out their lives for the sake of the flock, never taking a day off. We then exalt them as heroes instead of exposing them for their foolishness. We often do the same for the missionary who gives it all for the sake of the gospel on that foreign field. A person without rest is a person without wisdom. Overworking sounds right to our achievement-oriented culture, but God is unimpressed.

Many pastors lose years off of their lives by giving themselves to a busyness that violates how God made them. More times than not, it's a person searching for significance by being needed. The same can be said of business owners, educators, and the like. Many employees applaud their business owners who burn the candle at both ends; stockholders who see CEOs pour themselves out for the company's success are satisfied because it makes for quick financial gains. But it works against longevity, which is at the heart of a life of excellence. It'll cost us in the long run.

---

A person without rest is a person without wisdom. Overworking sounds right to our achievement-oriented culture, but God is unimpressed. *#bornforsignificance*

---

I realize this is often done sincerely. But drinking poison is harmful—even if you sincerely think it isn't. God has a way to do life. We are foolish to ignore it.

Excellence is the true life of significance. Anyone can have a high impact for a season. We see it in sports, politics, entertainment, and ministry. But only those who take care of themselves in a biblical fashion can leave a righteous momentum enjoyed by multiple generations. The idea of living for a generation we'll never see is what keeps us the most honest in our approach to life.

## DIVINE PERCEPTION

Such busyness hinders our perception of the things that are most important to God. Jesus taught us that our eye should be single. (See Matthew 6:22, KJV). The word *single* in this verse comes from two words: the number *one* and the word *voyage*. When the focus of our hearts has been refined to the one journey we're called to, everything about us comes under the influence of the light of God's presence/face. This is the life of significance, the life of ever-increasing favor, both from God and from man.

Favor is one of the most precious gifts that God gives to

people, believer and nonbeliever alike. Each person has a measure. Acts 14:17 attests to that: "Nevertheless He did not leave Himself without witness, in that He did good, gave us rain from heaven and fruitful seasons, filling our hearts with food and gladness" (NKJV). This is such a beautiful description of a perfect Father who woos people to Himself through His kindness and favor. I believe this process is still God's plan A for how to build His family, as it is still His "kindness that leads people to repentance" (Rom. 2:4).

## JESUS NEEDED FAVOR

Some biblical concepts are more of a mystery to me than others, and this would be toward the top of my list: Jesus, who was perfect in every way, needed to increase in favor with God and man. (See Luke 2:52.) I understand why Jesus needed to grow in favor with man. That favor would get Him into the Pharisee's home for a meal. It would enable Him to call to men mending their fishing nets, and they would leave everything to follow Him. Without increased favor with people, the impact of His life would have fallen far short of the Father's intent. But why does the One who is perfect in every way need to increase in favor with God, His own Father?

---

Blessings add to our lives; misused blessings subtract. *#bornforsignificance*

---

Jesus' birth was celebrated by angels, creation, people, and the Father Himself. Jesus was perfectly holy and entirely God, while also being entirely man. He was obedient in every way, eventually to the point of His own death. There were no blemishes in the least, nor were there any deficiencies. So why did

Jesus need to increase in favor with the Father? I don't know. But what I do know is that if Jesus needed it, I really need it. And all the more!

Each of us was born for significance. We were born for promotion, and stewarding favor well is at the core of the process of promotion. God has more significant designs for us than would naturally enter our hearts or minds. His plan really is beyond all we could ask or think. But there's a catch. Ill-used favor works against the very purpose for which it was given. Blessings add to our lives; misused blessings subtract.

Herein lies my favorite insight into the proper use of the gift called favor. The Queen of Sheba prophesied over Solomon with these words: "Blessed be the LORD your God who delighted in you to set you on the throne of Israel; because the LORD loved Israel forever, therefore He made you king, to do justice and righteousness" (1 Kings 10:9). This is one of the most important insights about promotion and favor. God had unusual favor on Solomon and gave him one of the ultimate promotions in position and personal experience of anyone ever to live. The reason for this unprecedented level of God's favor was that God loved Israel. This is stunning! God gives favor to individuals because of His love for those under their influence. The implication of this truth is significant: the favor upon our lives must be used to benefit those around us, or it is misused favor.

## KINGS MATTER TO GOD

We live at a time when people of means or position are the target of much malice, criticism, and suspicion. It's deserving in part. But only in a small part. Not everyone rises to high places of society and culture because of sin, manipulation, and robbery. Many people have started with humble means, but they obeyed

God and have risen to positions of rule, authority, and influence. God didn't promote them so they would fail. He did so because He entrusted them with the resources to lead and serve well.

God promoted them according to the promise of His Word. They deserve our respect and honor, if for no other reason than they were made in the image of God. It's interesting to note that many of them didn't even know they were obeying God when they made courageous decisions. They just responded to the wisdom that God had put in their hearts for their promotion. The gift came with the position.

The "kings of the earth"—the people of extraordinary influence—are the hardest to influence. And yet God cares for them as much as He does for the most broken among us. In fact, many of the richest in the world are the poorest inside—and they know it. But they also know that countless numbers of people would like to be their friends because they want something from them.

This challenge is recorded well in Proverbs 19.

> Wealth makes many friends, but the poor is separated from his friend…Many entreat the favor of the nobility, and every man is a friend to one who gives gifts. All the brothers of the poor hate him; How much more do his friends go far from him! He may pursue them with words, yet they abandon him.
>
> —PROVERBS 19:4, 6–7, NKJV

Proverbs, the book that equips us to reign in life, addresses the problem of touching royalty in ways that illustrate integrity. The phrase that stands out to me is that you might "stand before kings" (Prov. 22:29). There it is, God's desire. God has a method to promote the average person into a place of influence with those outside our typical circle of influence. This should capture the attention of us all, as this reveals a purpose for promotion: influence beyond reason.

Here are a few useful insights for understanding our purpose and process of promotion.

> The king's favor is toward a wise servant, but his wrath is against him who causes shame.
>
> —Proverbs 14:35, NKJV

Wisdom enables a servant/slave to have influence in the life of a king.

> Righteous lips are the delight of kings, and they love him who speaks what is right.
>
> —Proverbs 16:13, NKJV

The kings of the earth are attracted to people who speak things that are true, lovely, and of good report (Phil. 4:8). Don't mistake this for flattery, which is a poor counterfeit for the real thing. When we sense the heart of God for a person, it's important to speak it. Righteous lips are highly valued by everyone—especially kings.

My senior associate, Kris Vallotton, has mentioned on several occasions how he will be seated next to an atheist on a flight. Every time he lets them know that God has given him a word for them, they want to listen. Every time. It's in the heart of people to hear what God is saying, even though five minutes earlier, they denied He exists. It pulls them into their destiny.

It's no wonder kings delight in the words of the righteous. Those words restore their hearts and minds to the absolutes from which healthy governments rule. They become anchors in the storm of public opinion.

> Do you see a man who excels in his work? He will stand before kings; He will not stand before unknown men.
>
> —Proverbs 22:29, nkjv

This verse tells me three important things to understand. First, kings have an appetite for excellence. I believe it is a God-given appetite. This doesn't mean they always use it correctly. But it is there and should be acknowledged. Such a demand for excellence causes the workforce to create better and better products for the king to enjoy. This also helps the overall economy, as we learn to live at a higher level of excellence.

Second, it tells me that excellence is a key to promotion. Because we know that promotion comes from the Lord, we know that it is God who values excellence from us and uses it to increase and accelerate the measure of our influence.

But the third thing is easiest to miss: God gives us instruction on how to influence kings because it's His dream for us. It is in His heart for us to have a godly influence on those outside our social class. Jealousy won't accomplish that. Neither will dishonor, accusation, or anger. But honor will. When we use the gifts God has given us to be excellent in all things, God lifts the veil to increase our range of influence.

I consider excellence to be one of the three major expressions of wisdom in the Bible. The other two are creativity and integrity. More on this later.

## NO ONE IS FORGOTTEN

Nehemiah is one of the great heroes of the faith in Scripture. His courage, his level of sacrificial living, and his resolve to glorify God in everything are legendary. But he already had influence with kings. He was King Artaxerxes' cupbearer, which was a high-trust position. He was to protect the king from being poisoned. Nehemiah lived in luxury, similar to the king. He most likely resided in the palace with many of his own servants as well as had other benefits of wealth. Yet his heart was in Jerusalem, the once great city that had been destroyed.

---

Real promotion enables a person to see the purpose behind the seasons of unusual favor. *#bornforsignificance*

---

This great man had a heart for his people and his homeland. He fasted and prayed, crying out to God for the restoration of this wonderful city. After obtaining leave from his king, he led the rebuilding process with courage, boldness, amazing organizational skills, and the absolute resolve that nothing would hinder his assignment. His courage and vision fueled the whole process. But his generosity equally made this endeavor possible.

> Moreover, from the time that I was appointed to be their governor in the land of Judah, from the twentieth year until the thirty-second year of King Artaxerxes, twelve years, neither I nor my brothers ate the governor's provisions. But the former governors who were before me laid burdens on the people, and took from them bread and wine, besides forty shekels of silver. Yes, even their servants bore rule over the people, but I did not do so, because of the fear of God. Indeed, I also continued the work on this wall, and we did not buy any land. All my servants were gathered there for the work.
>
> And at my table were one hundred and fifty Jews and rulers, besides those who came to us from the nations around us. Now that which was prepared daily was one ox and six choice sheep. Also fowl were prepared for me, and once every ten days an abundance of all kinds of wine.

> Yet in spite of this I did not demand the governor's provisions, because the bondage was heavy on this people.
>
> Remember me, my God, for good, according to all that I have done for this people.
>
> —Nehemiah 5:14–19, nkjv

Nehemiah was a man of great resources who used them for a higher purpose than sitting in the king's palace and enjoying personal pleasure. It's not that personal pleasure is sin. Hardly. But real promotion enables a person to see the purpose behind the seasons of unusual favor. It's for the sake of others. And while kings matter to God, so do the homeless and broken. Nehemiah used what he had to serve the destiny of a nation, Israel. His beautiful use of favor put the people of God in a wonderful place of being restored to God's purposes as a nation. Favor used well will usually increase the favor of those who have been impacted. Favor and promotion are contagious.

Again, favor brings on increased responsibilities and often a refined focus for our purpose in life. And those who were to benefit most from Nehemiah's promotion were the Israelites. He was an inspiration to the people, as it was said they had a mind to work. I'm sure it was the fact that this wealthy representative of royalty got into the dirt himself and worked. His example of serving well inspired a level of devotion that had been previously unheard of, at least for this generation.

It can also be said that great favor inspires great opposition. "When Sanballat the Horonite and Tobiah the Ammonite official heard of it, they were deeply disturbed that a man had come to seek the well-being of the children of Israel" (Neh. 2:10, nkjv). With promotion often comes equal opposition.

## REFINED FOCUS

It's amazing how much we can see when we refine our focus. Perhaps this is why the enemy works so hard to keep us overextended in commitments and overfull schedules. It hinders our perception of reality. But there is clarity of heart and mind available to us when we have a refined focus consistent with our purpose.

One of the most exciting aspects of favor is that it automatically increases our opportunities to serve. Doors open left and right when there's a strong gift of favor on someone's life.

One of the harder lessons to learn in life is that favor will sometimes open doors we are not meant to walk through. Let me illustrate it this way: Let's say I have five opportunities to speak on the same date because of the favor on my life. Obviously, I can't be in more than one place at a time, so my challenge is twofold. Am I supposed to travel in ministry on that date? If so, where? I do believe God has a will for me in this dilemma. In other words, He has a specific assignment for me in my travels. All I want to do is honor Him, so my challenge is to find His heart and mind for this open door.

Let's say that after I pray for a while, I feel invitation number two is His will for my life. Does that mean that the other four opportunities were distractions sent by the devil? No. I don't believe that at all. Favor opens doors that I am not to go through, but I am to receive encouragement from them as tokens of God's favor upon my life. The fact that anyone would want me to come and speak somewhere is a great honor, and I must treat those opportunities as such.

## FAVOR HAS A REASON

It would be a wrong emphasis for me to say the only purpose of favor or blessings is to give them away. If I work hard to give an elaborate gift to my children, I don't want them to give it away. In other words, I didn't give them *seed* (to be planted through giving); I gave them *bread* (for personal consumption). Sometimes we grieve the Lord by our inability to receive the gift He's given us for our own enjoyment.

---

Favor is not given to us to improve our self-image. It is so we can represent Him well and address the issues of life that have brought death, loss, and destruction into society as a whole. *#bornforsignificance*

---

That being said, the reason for favor and blessing often goes beyond our personal lives. Favor must benefit the people under our influence, or there's a good chance it will be misused.

We find one of the best examples of increased favor in the story of Elijah and Elisha. While I'll cover more about them later, it's important to draw one element into the story line now. Favor is not given to us to improve our self-image. It is so we can represent Him well and address the issues of life that have brought death, loss, and destruction into society as a whole. We must deal with these things in Jesus' name. Favor is the ability to use His name well and see His will done on earth as it is in heaven.

## CHAPTER 3

# REIGNING IN LIFE

Our journey to discovering our God-given significance has revealed that all promotion, favor, and blessing are to enable us to succeed in this one overarching assignment: reigning in life. This is a subject that I have been referring to and will continue to mention throughout this book. But in this chapter, I'll approach it as a primary theme, giving bite-sized pieces on the topic.

God designed us to reign in life. Think of it, the master planner, the designer of all, wrote into our DNA that we should reign. Many react to that kind of statement because it seems to say that we are to seek to be exalted. Self-exaltation is a poor counterfeit for reigning in life, which ultimately is living according to the plan, purpose, and design of God. He is exalted when all He made functions according to His will, design, and purpose. And we were made to live in His glory, illustrating His likeness in all we do.

Our understanding of royalty is skewed and is what makes the idea of *reigning* sound offensive. And yet I remind you, Jesus is a King—the King of all kings, in fact. Royalty isn't a bad concept; it's just been poorly represented in the earth. We have the chance to set the record straight by how the church is blessed, giving all for the benefit of others.

## THE BOOK

Much of what we are to learn on this subject comes from Proverbs, the book known for wisdom. The word *proverb* has as its root meaning to rule or reign. The purpose of wisdom is to enable us to reign in life, and Brian Simmons of The Passion Translation told me that understanding this concept is the key to understanding the Book of Proverbs. I agree completely. That one statement put into place the purpose behind years of reading and studying that book.

---

Think of it, the master planner, the designer of all, wrote into our DNA that we should reign. *#bornforsignificance*

---

And lest anyone think *reigning in life* to be an Old Testament concept only, it is repeated in what is often considered the ultimate theological book of the Bible, Romans.

> For if by the one man's offense death reigned through the one, much more those who receive abundance of grace and of the gift of righteousness will *reign in life* through the One, Jesus Christ.
>
> —Romans 5:17, nkjv

The Passion Translation puts Romans 5:17 this way:

> Death once held us in its grip, and by the blunder of one man, death reigned as king over humanity. But now, how much more are we held in the grip of grace and continue *reigning as kings in life*, enjoying our regal freedom

> through the gift of perfect righteousness in the one and only Jesus, the Messiah!

The King James Version of the Bible uses the word *promotion* in Psalm 75:6–7, saying, "Promotion comes from the Lord." It is probably the most well-known scripture on the subject. A high percentage of the other translations use the word *exalted* or *exaltation* or something similar.

> For exaltation comes neither from the east nor from the west nor from the south. But God is the Judge: *He* puts down one, and *exalts another.*
>
> —PSALM 75:6–7, NKJV

The point is, thinking of people being exalted is offensive to some who think only of God being exalted. But promotion, or exaltation, is connected to God's sovereignty and His justice. This passage introduces Him as the judge, who has complete liberty to put one down and exalt another. Another way to put this is promotion is an expression of God's justice. To deny it in efforts of false humility is to deny His justice.

It is vital that we accept His promotions as well as His delays. He is God, and He is exalted by His choices. Yielding to them is wisdom.

> Let not mercy and truth forsake you; bind them around your neck, write them on the tablet of your heart, and so find *favor and high esteem in the sight of God and man.*
>
> —PROVERBS 3:3–4, NKJV

Mercy and truth are a great combination of kingdom values. It reminds me of the New Testament admonition, "Speak the truth in love" (Eph. 4:15, NLT). Truth without love can be brutal. Love without truth changes nothing. Grouping the two ensures we are functioning for the sake of others, not just our need to vent when we see what is wrong.

In the case of Proverbs 3:3–4, the commitment to mercy, which is the loving-kindness patiently shown to another, would be readily embraced. This then is seasoned with the medicinal qualities of truth so people find answers from us, not just comfort in their problems. What's interesting about the favor mentioned here is that it is with God and man. That's exactly what happened to Jesus. He grew in favor with God and man.

> *Wisdom* is the principal thing; therefore get wisdom. And in all your getting, get understanding. Exalt her, and *she will promote you; she will bring you honor*, when you embrace her.
>
> —Proverbs 4:7–8, nkjv

---

Truth without love can be brutal. Love without truth changes nothing. Grouping the two ensures we are functioning for the sake of others. *#bornforsignificance*

---

Wisdom is the basis for promotion in the kingdom. God looks for occasion to promote and give honor to His children. He loves everyone unconditionally, but it would be foolish to think we all have the same measure of favor. In a very real sense, the favor on our lives is determined by what we have done with the love we have received. And regardless of what we started with, favor increases through faithful use.

> Hear instruction and be wise, and do not disdain it. For whoever finds me finds life, and *obtains favor* from the Lord; but he who sins against me wrongs his own soul; all those who hate me love death.
>
> —Proverbs 8:33, 35–36, nkjv

Wisdom is said to be more valuable than gold and silver. I only know I believe that *if my pursuit of wisdom actually cost me something*. It's more than an inspirational statement; it is a value that shapes life. And when wisdom is valued the way God intended, He extends His scepter of favor over that life. Wisdom attracts divine favor, which is more valuable than all riches.

> By the blessing of the upright the city is exalted, but it is overthrown by the mouth of the wicked.
>
> —Proverbs 11:11, nkjv

When those who live righteously are blessed enough to be a blessing, a city receives its promotion. God still thinks in terms of cities and nations. And the well-being of those who follow Jesus can mark a city for blessing and eternal purpose. Conversely, the mouths of the wicked will rob a city of its potential promotion by the damage done through the ideas, ambitions, and values revealed in their speech. Truly, life and death are in the power of the tongue. The righteous must make godly decrees over our cities in order for them to reach their God-given potential.

> The *generous* soul will be made *rich*, and he who waters will also be watered himself. The people will curse him who withholds grain, but *blessing* will be on the head of him *who sells it*.
>
> —Proverbs 11:25–26, nkjv

This verse is a personal favorite because Solomon doesn't do what we'd expect. The subject is generosity, a highly valued kingdom virtue. But while he honors the generous, we expect him to say the one who grows grain should give it away. And while there is a place for that, Solomon declares the blessing and favor of God comes upon the one who sells it to the citizens of his community. This is astonishing! Generosity is likened to working hard in our assignment in life, making a product that benefits people around us, and then selling it. Using our skills, gifts, and resources to benefit others is honored by God. If I grow a crop and you buy it and have food, God calls me generous. I have become a contributor to your life and, in a broader sense, to society. Making a profit for my family's benefit is not evil. In fact, this process is honored by the Lord. It's what makes for healthy communities.

> He who earnestly seeks good finds favor, but trouble will come to him who seeks evil.
>
> —Proverbs 11:27, nkjv

The pursuit of our lives in thought, ambition, and plans determines the measure of favor we will enjoy in life. The word *good* here means pleasant and agreeable. Those who prioritize their role in benefiting others socially will find favor throughout their lives.

> He who trusts in his riches will fall, but the righteous will flourish like foliage.
>
> —Proverbs 11:28, nkjv

It's very interesting that those who trust in riches fall, but those who live righteously flourish. The implication is that they're righteous because of their trust in God. While *to flourish* is not limited to money, it certainly includes it.

> A good man obtains favor from the Lord, but a man of wicked intentions He will condemn.
>
> —Proverbs 12:2, nkjv

This is such a beautiful verse as it deals with the simpler parts of a person's makeup and personality. Here the word *good* means pleasant, friendly, kind, and joyful. If you own a restaurant and you're looking to hire or even promote someone, the person who is kind and friendly will probably be your choice. We instinctively know the answer to that one. But this verse is saying that the promotion you, the owner, give to that person, the employee, is actually from the Lord. God is the One who highlighted and honored the one who chose to live in such a way that they were a social benefit to those around them. They bring an emotional wealth to others.

> Good understanding gains favor, but the way of the unfaithful is hard.
>
> —Proverbs 13:15, nkjv

It's interesting that understanding, which is always according to what God says and thinks, attracts favor. We see this illustrated in the story of the centurion in Matthew 8:8–13. This soldier wanted his servant healed. When he revealed his understanding of how authority worked and his confidence that Jesus could perform the miracle, Jesus was stopped in his tracks. Kingdom understanding gives way to faith. As a result, the centurion was granted the miracle he asked for. Truly, understanding gains favor. Whenever God sees we have given ourselves to understand from His perspective, the only authentic one, He gives us favor.

> The king's favor is toward a wise servant, but his wrath is against him who causes shame.
>
> —Proverbs 14:35, nkjv

Even servants can increase in favor with mankind, including royalty, if they live with wisdom. Wisdom is one of the most common ways of obtaining favor and promotion for our lives. Because this was mentioned for a servant, it basically says that no position is so low that wisdom won't benefit you, nor so far removed from people that you will go unnoticed.

> He who finds a wife finds a good thing, and obtains favor from the Lord.
>
> —Proverbs 18:22, nkjv

I don't believe this is saying if you merely get married, you have favor. Anyone can get a marriage license but miss out entirely on the favor granted in this journey. By implication, I believe this is saying that anyone who joins with another to become one—and in doing so displays the covenant of God with mankind—favor is increased in that person's life.

The relational component for our lives is valuable to God. This is where we demonstrate who we really are. If we are not relationally connected to others, we can live under the illusion that we abound in the fruits of the Spirit. Besides, our relationship with God is measured in our relationships with others.

> A good name is to be chosen rather than great riches, loving favor rather than silver and gold.
>
> —Proverbs 22:1, nkjv

People often choose personal gain, as it pertains to money or position, at the expense of favor. Favor, much like wisdom, is the prize. Choosing wealth, at the expense of favor, is short-lived. But choosing favor over wealth often results in greater wealth than if it had been the priority. Solomon's middle-of-the-night encounter illustrates this idea quite well. He chose, out of the favor of the moment, something that benefited others. And he ended up with all the other things he could have asked for.

> But those who rebuke the wicked will have delight, and a good blessing will come upon them.
>
> —Proverbs 24:25, NKJV

Here's one of the more surprising places to obtain favor and blessings. It's when we rebuke the wicked. Being silent when things are going horribly wrong, in a societal context, isn't right. We must speak. It attracts God's favor and blessings.

---

If it doesn't hurt to correct someone, don't do it...Keep quiet, at least until you can feel the heart of God for the other. *#bornforsignificance*

---

Let me pause for a moment because even as I write this, I can see many who are now thankful they have biblical permission to correct everyone around them who needs fixing! A friend of mine helped me with this idea over forty years ago. He told me if it doesn't hurt to correct someone, don't do it. If there's pleasure or merely the chance to vent all your feelings, keep quiet, at least until you can feel the heart of God for the other. That has been a healthy standard for me all these years.

> When the righteous are in authority, the people rejoice; but when a wicked man rules, the people groan.
>
> —Proverbs 29:2, NKJV

Wicked rulers are cruel. Righteous leaders give reason for joy. The wicked demands and puts down. The righteous empowers and honors. As previously stated, the two basic reasons for government of any kind are ruling to protect and serving to empower. When the righteous are promoted, people are aching for someone who will celebrate and empower them into their destiny. This is what the righteous must do well.

> The fear of man brings a snare, but he who trusts in the Lord will be exalted.
>
> —Proverbs 29:25

Our ability to trust in God is contrasted with the fear of man. And rightly so. Wherever the fear of man has a voice, there is weak trust in God. You can only fear one or the other, God or man. And the one you fear is the one you will instinctively trust when that moment of testing or opportunity comes.

## ROYAL PRIESTHOOD

We are called to royalty. But it is royalty from God's perspective. Priests are those who minister to God and to man. A royal priesthood is made up of those who use their place of favor before God to help and assist people.

Anyone who thinks reigning in life means ruling over people just needs to picture the King of all kings washing the disciples' feet. Here we see the highest One doing the lowest deed. The point is, we are to use whatever means God has given us to benefit others. All positions of rule need to be embraced with humility.

Our power is for others. But there are times when it is also with great firmness. This is when our responsibility is to bring protection. I remember once when my son Eric was small, he was outside playing in our yard. A strange man made his way onto our property, accompanied by a mutual friend. From the man's crazed behavior, I immediately sensed that he was under heavy demonic influence. He displayed some aggressive behavior toward Eric, which I intercepted immediately. Obviously, my first responsibility was the protection of my son. I positioned myself between Eric and this man in case anything would go haywire. There was no timidity on my part. Neither was there any need to appear humble. My role of ruling, in this case, was to protect.

We must remember in life that we are to take our positions of rule out of our God-given responsibility and make sure it is not for position or title but is for the benefit of others. This can and must be done with kindness wherever possible—even toward the demonized man. It was.

To serve with the heart of a king automatically implies vast resources and noble intentions. This is the joy of serving in the kingdom of God. We do so with the unlimited resources of the King of all kings. Carrying this into our place of service brings great joy and honor to those being served. You never want to make others feel your act of service is wearisome. The heart of a king, the place of rich identity in God, will help keep us from that error.

Every assignment in life is an invitation to excellence, creativity, and integrity. These are the hallmarks of achievement for the believer; they truly express the wisdom of God. The external parts of life are only window dressing. To live wisely is to reign in life.

## CHAPTER 4

# THE FORCE OF HOLY DESIRE

DESIRE IS A powerful component that shapes the destiny and significance of life in many ways. Desire in and of itself is neither good nor bad. It can lead to devastation and the breakdown of all that is good in the world, or it can lead to significance, breakthrough, and countless solutions for the human condition. It can be as simple as what we want to eat for lunch or as complex as the dream of establishing a space station on Mars. On the other end of the spectrum, it is the birthplace of the most destructive influences in the earth, with the most horrible social sins as its fruit. It is the driving force behind all human achievements, both good and bad.

The condition of our hearts determines the impact that desire has on our lives. Our having desires that testify of who God is and how we are designed is the target of the Lord. When He created us with a free will, He did so to illustrate that it is possible to have those made in the image of God who worship Him by choice. Our desires either reveal God or undermine the message of His love and vision for humanity. But desire is here to stay, and we must use this force to His advantage.

## UNHOLY RELIGION

Religion has a great effect on our desires. To clarify, I usually use the term *religion* in a negative context, although it can be used in a positive way. In this setting, *religion* is form without power; it is routine without relationship. Simply put, it is the number one killer of our ability to dream. Intentionally so. The enemy, who inspires this type of religion, wants us to settle for anything inferior. It is possible to be involved in a form of the gospel that's just enough to ease our conscience. In doing so, we become satisfied with the inferior; we settle for form without power. For example, truth from His Word is to lead us to Him. But many are satisfied with good theology and stop short of an encounter with the One to whom the Scriptures are pointing.

---

The condition of our hearts determines the impact that desire has on our lives. Our desires either reveal God or undermine the message of His love and vision for humanity. *#bornforsignificance*

---

Many believers are unwilling to let desires form in their hearts because they're afraid of getting it wrong. They can recite well the passages that speak of self-denial. They continue by explaining that the absence of a dream is the product of bearing their cross. Unfortunately for all of us, they have a personal cross without a personal resurrection.

The enemy fears what would happen if we discovered the power of sanctified desires. His goal is to keep us blind to an unexplainable invitation by Jesus to dream. Four times in three chapters (John 14–16) Jesus invites His disciples to ask for whatever they want.

Understand that Jesus wasn't inviting us to develop our bent toward being selfish and then call it spiritual. But neither was He asking us to robotically repeat preprogrammed prayers. He was inviting us into the ultimate relational journey with fulfilled desires as the fruit of the relationship. Think of it, the fruit of our walk with God is answered prayer that reveals Him to the nations. That is significance on a rarely-thought-of level.

The tree of life, He calls it, is what we were born for. It is found in our beginning in the Garden of Eden in Genesis chapters 2 and 3. It is also found in Proverbs, in the book that trains us to reign in life, and then in Revelation. The tree of life is in our past, our present, and our future. My favorite use of this phrase is found in Proverbs.

> Hope deferred makes the heart sick, but when the desire comes, it is a tree of life.
>
> —Proverbs 13:12, nkjv

The tree of life, in a very real sense, connects us to our eternal purpose. After the sin of Adam and Eve eating the forbidden fruit, an angel protected them from eating from the tree of life. It is commonly thought that eating from that tree would make their sinful condition eternal, without a solution, so the angel protected them from making sinfulness their eternal condition. And yet wisdom opens up the subject for us in a new way, letting us see that His intent is our having fulfilled desires. And that fulfillment was like eating from the tree of life.

Thus, our eternal purpose is found in the partnership we are to have with God, where our desires move Him into action on our behalf. The picture is of a tree that bears fruit from which we feed ourselves. And that fruit is fulfilled desires. It's interesting that the same principle is addressed in John 15:7–8:

> If you abide in Me, and My words abide in you, ask *whatever you wish*, and it will be done for you. My Father is glorified by this, that you *bear much fruit*, and so prove to be My disciples.

And then in John 15:16:

> You did not choose Me but I chose you, and appointed you that you would *go and bear fruit*, and that your fruit would remain, so that *whatever you ask* of the Father in My name *He may give to you.*

Of course, our fruitfulness must be seen in the character of Christ established in our lives. But there are many nice people who accomplish little for eternity in Jesus' name. Our fruitfulness in life must also be measured by our answers to prayer. We have to look at it this way: Prayer is not where we try to convince God of anything. We must love His will and be unimpressed with ours. This privileged position is where His heart and His will become our own, and our partnership is revealed through prayer.

---

The enemy fears what would happen if we discovered the power of sanctified desires. *#bornforsignificance*

---

If I own a house but decide to rent it to another family, it is still entirely mine. Yet although I own the home, I cannot enter it whenever I want to, even if I have my own master key to the front door. It is illegal for me to enter. I have to be invited to go into my own home.

It's the same here on earth. The earth is the Lord's, but He planted us here as delegated authority. He responds to the prayers of His people. In a sense, we give Him an invitation to come and do as He pleases.

John Wesley said, "God does nothing except in response to believing prayer." I don't have the right to say what God can and cannot do. He is God. He alone has that right. He is the One who invited us into a relationship where what we desire in the earth is what happens in the earth. Sometimes He answers our prayer and acts on our behalf. Other times He would rather do something through us instead of for us.

## NO MISTAKES HERE

The fear of getting the issue of desires wrong has paralyzed many. It is true that parked cars get no speeding tickets. But the car wasn't made to be still. It was designed to move. So it is with the hearts and minds of men and women around the world. A sign of being truly alive is having the ability and freedom to dream.

> People do not despise a thief if he steals to satisfy himself when he is starving. Yet when he is found, he must restore sevenfold; He may have to give up all the substance of his house.
>
> —Proverbs 6:30–31, nkjv

This verse fascinates me. Thieves are not despised if they stole to satisfy hunger, the most basic condition of humanity. Stealing is still not approved of here, nor are they off the hook for their crime. It's just that people understand the nature of some desires is right, and some desires are even noble. Such is the case of a starving man. He still must restore what was taken, but society understands his desire for food.

While that most basic need for food may stand out to most, I'd like to suggest that the freer a person becomes in Christ, the more he or she is able to desire right things with a similar appetite to a starving man. Discovering who we are as children of the Creator aligns our thinking to being creative. In many cases, it is appropriate to suggest that the desire of someone to create or design is similar to the desire for the most basic needs of life, such as food. There are few things as rewarding in life as when we sense God has taken delight in our desires. The ultimate partnership then takes place, as we discover the fullest manifestation of being co-laborers.

> For you were called to freedom, brethren; only do not turn your freedom into an opportunity for the flesh, but through love serve one another.
>
> —Galatians 5:13

Even our freedoms are to benefit those around us. To use our freedom only for ourselves is to miss the reason it was given. So then, this verse is saying that freedom is given to us by God. But we must be intentional in the way we use this gift. It must benefit others, or it is misused.

---

Prayer is not where we try to convince God of anything. We must love His will and be unimpressed with ours. This privileged position is where His heart and His will become our own, and our partnership is revealed through prayer. *#bornforsignificance*

---

I find self-discovery to be quite boring. But discovering Him has opened up my heart and mind to see who He made me to be. And once again, anyone who has discovered who God made them to be will never want to be someone else.

## CULTURAL HEROES

I love reading about some of the leaders of innovation throughout history. It appears to me that their need to create was as strong as most people's hunger for food. Nikola Tesla, Winston Churchill, and Steve Jobs come to mind. It was as if they had been chosen by God to solve a crisis, end a war, or design something that would advance society at an alarming rate. To say they were possessed rightfully carries negative implications because of the stories of demonized people in the Bible. And yet it seems in some ways like a fitting description, obviously without the devil present, when we read of how they could barely sleep or eat until their idea was fully realized or their plan and strategy were in full operation.

George Frideric Handel's story of writing the musical masterpiece *Messiah* is an excellent example of this explosive discovery of purpose. He hardly ate or slept during the twenty-four days of writing what many consider the greatest piece of music ever written. Perhaps the greatest musical accomplishment of all time happened because there was burning in the heart of a man not known for his spirituality. It's as though he was chosen for this task, and it was then birthed in him. It was in him, and it had to get out.

The famed *Hallelujah Chorus* was his crowning touch. This he wrote under divine fervor, saying, he "saw all of heaven" before him. He ended his work with the inscription *Soli Deo Gloria*, meaning "to God alone the glory." Stunning. I'm glad the religious crowd didn't get to him first and cut off his capacity to dream. We would all be poorer for it.

We were designed to desire. We were born to create. We were made to pursue and apprehend. To ignore these God-given parts of our lives is to deny our design, and in a measure, the nature of our designer imparted to us. In the same way, the Holy Spirit is known for bringing freedom to a person's life, so religious *routine without relationship* brings restriction and confinement. The worst part of that equation is that people in that bondage take delight in sacrificing their desires to prove that they are true disciples of Jesus. We need godly dreamers now more than ever.

## JESUS, THE DESIGNER OF DESIRE

It fascinates me that twelve guys who grew up in the most insignificant setting, with the most mundane jobs and boring family legacies, would wake up to their capacity to dream when they started following Jesus. Their devotion to this dream was so intense that they often thought they might have to die to protect it. He had that effect on people.

---

I find self-discovery to be quite boring. But discovering Him has opened up my heart and mind to see who He made me to be. *#bornforsignificance*

---

Admittedly, they desired to be better than each other, they wanted exclusive rights to Jesus, and they wished to call down fire and kill an entire city. It's all found in Luke 9. But these are wrong desires, you say. Of course they are. But look at Jesus' response. He never tried to kill their ability to dream or their capacity to desire. Their wants needed refinement, redefinition, and redirection. But He did not kill their capacity to dream. Nor did He criticize their personal passion for greatness. He simply redefined it according to the perspective of the kingdom. Liberty restores the capacity to dream.

When they argued as to who was the greatest among them,

Jesus pointed to the servant and called that one great. Another time He pointed to a child and called the child great. The point is, He didn't rebuke their desire for significance. He just pruned it into a shape that would fit nicely in His kingdom.

## LONGING FOR MORE

Most of us quite naturally long for promotion. Whether it is in our prayer life, our jobs, our incomes, our gifts and ministries, or the favor given to our families, it is natural to hunger for more. I think it's potentially one of the most unselfish and Christlike desires we can have. In every place I've traveled in the world, people are wired this way. Whether they live in oceanfront mansions, mud huts, or garbage dumps, all try to improve their lives. Some of the poorest will even show their passion for improvement by hanging a picture on their wall that they found discarded at the dump. Or they'll spend time sweeping their dirt floor. The desire for excellence is in all of us in measure. In a very real sense, we are all born for significance.

As believers, we must champion the cause of those around us for greatness and significance. As we speak the Word of the Lord over them, we just might help them fully discover who God made them to be. We have found that many people become tender toward the Lord once they see that He really cares about what they care about. I have found that if it matters to me, it matters to God. More people need to know this about Him. The fruitfulness of our lives must reveal this truth.

Have you ever prayed big prayers? For me the big prayers are for our entire city to be saved, for everyone I pray for to get healed, to see revival change our country, and to see nations discipled in my lifetime. Such prayers are usually prayed because they are in the heart of God first. It is the deep of God calling to the deep in us. He inspires the desires that give way to such prayers.

The answers to prayers of this nature are, in some ways, the greatest expressions of personal promotion. It's not our titles or accomplishments; it's our significance, the impact of our lives. For me personally, my dream is not to have a big church. Instead, I want to raise up big people—people who live out of their significance before God.

---

I have found that if it matters to me, it matters to God. More people need to know this about Him. *#bornforsignificance*

---

The answers to prayers that release the almighty God into the affairs of man are the greatest example of significance and promotion. How can one even imagine anything greater than being a co-laborer with God? He invites us into significance.

> For not from the east, nor from the west, nor from the desert comes exaltation; But God is the Judge; He puts down one and exalts another.
>
> —Psalm 75:6–7

Promotion comes from God. Period. No man is big enough to stand in the way of someone God wants to promote. Yielding to His purposes makes us candidates to be involved in His process. It is also true that He puts down those who are proud. Humility is, once again, the ingredient that keeps us the safest.

Here's the bottom line: answers to prayer reveal God in the earth. I can't think of a better way to achieve significance than to help people more fully see who Jesus is and discover the incredible love of a perfect Father. This happens when our prayers are answered.

## THE PROMISED LAND

We were born for increase, advancement, and significance. The Old Testament provides us with a great picture of this process when Israel entered and took possession of the Promised Land. The New Testament equivalent is of the believer entering the realities of the kingdom here and now. We do so by embracing the promises of God, contending for their fulfillment, thus letting them reveal our destinies.

The children of Israel had been slaves for a long time when Moses came to set them free. If ever there was a group of people who found it difficult to dream, we would probably agree it would be slaves, especially when those slaves had been in that condition for generations. Imagine what happened when God gave them a promise about a land where not only would they no longer be slaves, but they would be the masters of their own destinies. They would be the owners of blessed lands with abundant crops, and each family was to receive a wonderful inheritance. At first, it must have been hard to believe. But soon the capacity to dream was awakened, and they began to move toward fulfillment. The promises of God awaken us to our design. We come alive with hope and promise in order to reveal Him well.

Some scholars have counted more than seven thousand promises in the Bible. Each of them is an invitation to a relational journey where we discover the heart of God for people and planet earth. When God gives us a promise, He is expecting us to use it as a weapon to help bring about His purposes in and through our lives. It is true that He can—and sometimes will—bring about a fulfillment of a promise without our involvement.

But we learn little pertaining to our authority and responsibility this way. God designed the prophetic promises of Scripture to be our weapons, through which we help to bring about our entrance into His promised land.

This really is the lesson the apostle Paul provides for Timothy in 1 Timothy 1:17. He instructs him to use the prophecies as weapons. This implies that there is a conflict between the fulfillment of the promise and where I am in the moment. I have a responsibility to help bring the fulfillment about through the proper use of His promise. Simply declaring what God has said in the face of opposition is often where the breakthrough comes.

The Old Testament example of the Promised Land is one of the most understandable and inspirational stories in the Bible. In it are the examples of promise, conflict, the purifying process, healthy community life, prosperity, and overall well-being. It became the prototype of what God still has planned for the believer today.

---

When God gives us a promise, He is expecting us to use it as a weapon to help bring about His purposes in and through our lives. *#bornforsignificance*

---

However, we also have a great example of the will of God, New Testament style.

> First of all, then, I urge that entreaties and prayers, petitions and thanksgivings, be made on behalf of all men, for kings and all who are in authority, *so that we may lead a tranquil and quiet life* in all godliness and dignity. This is good and acceptable in the sight of God our Savior, *who desires all men to be saved* and to come to the knowledge of the truth.
>
> —1 Timothy 2:1–4

The prayer directions that God set forth for us are to set the stage for cities of peace to rule the day. It is in the heart of God for us to lead lives of peace. He gave us instructions on how to bring this about because of His dream for the earth to be filled with these kinds of communities. This reality is not dependent on the return of Jesus. It's dependent on the obedience of His people. The Passion Translation puts it this way: "that we would be able to live tranquil, undisturbed lives, as we worship the awe-inspiring God with pure hearts." I believe this to be a picture of the *city set on a hill* that attracts people into the community of the redeemed. This example of reigning in life is used as a tool by God to bring people to faith in Christ.

## REMOVING THE FEAR OF FAILURE

Many fear these promises being fulfilled in our day because they produce complacency. There's no doubt this is a possibility. But if we live our lives refusing to consider the possibilities of Scripture because of potential failure, we have already failed. Such lifestyles are based on fear and not promise. We become like the man with one talent who was afraid of losing his master's money, so he did nothing but hide it in order to protect it. That is the most dangerous position to be in. When we fear failure more than we fear the lack of success, we become protectors of doctrine instead of explorers of truth.

The possibilities contained in the promises of Scripture are our opportunity to illustrate the heart and nature of God to the nations. Possible failure cannot rule the day. Humility, accountability, and the willingness to risk all for His glory are the mandates of the hour. This story, along with many others in Scripture, is unto the salvation of nations.

This is the purpose of our significance: to become all that

God intended that we might serve effectively and illustrate well what God intended for all those made in the image of God. The salvation of nations is at stake. We serve that all would be touched by God, and we reign that all might thrive discovering God's desire for an abundant life of freedom and creative fulfillment for all. This is why we have been chosen, *for such a time as this.*

---

When we fear failure more than we fear the lack of success, we become protectors of doctrine instead of explorers of truth. *#bornforsignificance*

---

The plans for us are so grand that without the process of God, we would be ill-equipped for what He intends to do. Embracing the process and its purpose is the opportunity given to all in this next section.

# PART II

# THE PROCESS OF PROMOTION

## CHAPTER 5

# THE WAYS OF PROGRESS

Everything that Jesus taught and practiced spoke of forward motion and progress. It is His nature, *from glory to glory*. And it is how we were designed. Knowing this truth deep in our hearts should position us quite securely in our purpose so we never violate our design and merely occupy space.

While I strongly believe in the Lord's return, I also think many have become irresponsible in their assignment because of their anticipation of His return. Please read this carefully. The return of Jesus will be wonderful! But it is the hope of the church, not the hope of the world. The hope of the world is the power of the gospel. And it must be preached, lived, and demonstrated for it to become the ultimate invitation for all to come and discover this irresistible grace that leads to salvation.

### THE TOOLS FOR ADVANCEMENT

Our progress in the kingdom usually comes in one of two ways: by receiving or by apprehending. Both are essential lessons in learning the ways of progress or forward motion. The purpose behind each process is according to what God is building in us. Consider these Scriptures:

> Truly I say to you, whoever does not receive the kingdom of God like a child will not enter it at all.
>
> —Mark 10:15

> And from the days of John the Baptist until now the kingdom of heaven suffers violence, and the violent take it by force.
>
> —Matthew 11:12, nkjv

Together these Scriptures address the two primary ways we grow and make progress in the ways of the kingdom of God. Such advancements are promotions of sorts. God is the ultimate steward, who gives to us extravagantly but does so according to what we can successfully manage.

---

The return of Jesus will be wonderful! But it is the hope of the church, not the hope of the world. The hope of the world is the power of the gospel. *#bornforsignificance*

---

**1. Receiving at rest**

The first passage addresses what it is like to *receive* the kingdom. Interestingly, we can only enter in according to the measure we have received. To receive is to yield. It is how we start in the faith. "But as many as received Him, to them He gave the right to become children of God, even to those who believe in His name" (John 1:12). It's remarkable that receiving who God is and how He is to reign over us enables us to enter into all He has for us. To enter is how we walk out our faith in practical yet powerful ways. What we receive determines how we walk. It is vital to recognize the context in which things are received: *like a child.* He never wants the weightiness of what

He gives us in promotion to break what He has already built within us through our growth.

This method of increase and promotion is significant in that it spotlights who we are as children of God: heirs. Identity as a son or daughter is the focal point in this process. It's all about inheritance. Learning to receive as a child is about resting in who He says we are, and whose we are. The emphasis is not on what we can do to obtain what we've asked for; this part of the journey is all about what God has done for us. Childlikeness is highly valued in the kingdom of God.

Beni and I have had foster children several times in our married life. The most tragic story was of two boys whose mother and father had killed themselves within about a year of each other. They lived in extreme tension and abuse. To say they were damaged by their environment is an understatement. On top of that, they had been separated from their brothers, five of them in all, as they became wards of the state.

The first evening they were with us was interesting. We sat around the dinner table and began to pass the food. They grabbed all they could and protected it by wrapping their arms around their plates filled with food. It was easy to see that they were unsure of when they would eat again. We assured them they could have all they wanted, that no one would be taking their food, and there would be more food tomorrow. They soon realized there would be plenty, and they no longer had to fight for something to eat.

This illustrates a powerful point: orphans respond differently to the issues of life than do sons and daughters—than do heirs. These boys were orphans in heart long before their parents' suicides. The orphaned heart can't understand or discover the joy of receiving what the Father has already laid aside for enjoyment and pleasure. Anxiety in the heart comes from a damaged self-identity. Whenever there's a wrong identity of self, there's a wrong understanding of God, as we were made in His likeness.

Receiving as a child is all about knowing we are a child of the Father, with Jesus as our elder brother, who obtained an inheritance for us. He did the work. We do the receiving. It is the ultimate position of rest, void of all anxiety. Anxiety is a complete waste of time and energy.

**2. Apprehending at war**

I purpose *not* to live devil-conscious, because he is not worthy of my attention. But to live ignorant of the battle we have been called to is to live in the worst kind of denial. We were born into a war. Avoiding this reality is not an option for anyone who wants to grow in Christ.

> From the days of John the Baptist until now the kingdom of heaven suffers violence, and violent men take it by force.
>
> —MATTHEW 11:12

This second passage implies violence. Not against people, of course, as we've learned that the enemy of our souls is spiritual, living in the unseen realm. "For our struggle is not with flesh and blood" (Eph. 6:12). When we take something by force, we are fulfilling His command for us to use His authority to carry out His commission.

---

Learning to receive as a child is about resting in who He says we are, and whose we are. The emphasis is not on what we can do to obtain what we've asked for; [it's] about what God has done for us. *#bornforsignificance*

---

Where the first tool for advancement deals with our identity as children of God, this one is about our being a soldier in His army. Instead of the phrase "soldier in His army," we could say "responsible citizen of His kingdom." Either way, the focus is on our authority, which is to be used to obtain realms in God and to set people free. Apprehending things in the kingdom means we're willing and able to use the promises of God against all opposing forces that we might enter fully into all God intended for us.

Again, this is the New Testament equivalent of Israel's entering the Promised Land in the Old Testament. Israel faced enemy nations on the way to their fulfilled promise. It required them to act according to God's word to them.

God only leads us into a conflict that He's equipped us to win. Israel was once redirected around a clash because God knew they weren't ready for battle.

> Now when Pharaoh had let the people go, God did not lead them by the way of the land of the Philistines, even though it was near; for God said, "The people might change their minds when they see war, and return to Egypt." Hence God led the people around by the way of the wilderness to the Red Sea; and the sons of Israel went up in martial array from the land of Egypt.
>
> —Exodus 13:17–18

God trains and equips us for war and then arranges a conflict. It's not cruelty or punishment for us. It's a part of our training for eternity to rule and reign in Christ. Besides, this is an expression of the original commission found in Genesis 1:28, "Subdue the earth." It appears that when the devil was cast out of heaven, he ended up on planet earth, which explains how the earth could be under the influence of the powers of darkness when Adam and Eve were put in the Garden. They were given authority as the delegated authority of God to expel those powers. Although they failed their initial assignment, Jesus has restored us to that purpose, as revealed in the Great Commission. (See Matthew 28:19.)

This process is mighty through the proper use of the Word of God. His Word reveals His heart, His nature, and His promises. These are tools used in this triumphant assignment. This beautiful story of God leading Israel away from battle shows His wisdom to guide us only into conflicts for which we are ready.

## PURSUING THE BATTLE

Oftentimes we really don't know what kind of promotion is on our lives until we confront a problem. Sometimes problems are brought to us as natural parts of life, but other times we have to pursue them, as in the case of Elisha. For those of you unfamiliar with the story, Elisha was a servant to Elijah, the great prophet. Elisha was being mentored by his spiritual father in the prophetic. When it came time for Elijah to die, Elisha asked for a double portion of anointing on his own life as compared to Elijah's.

---

God's Word reveals His heart, His nature, and His promises. These are tools used in this triumphant assignment. *#bornforsignificance*

---

I encourage you to read all of this beautiful story, but for the purpose of this book, I want to focus on the part where Elijah came to a river with Elisha at his side. He then struck the waters with his mantle, which caused them to part. *Mantle* is another word for cloak. Elijah's mantle was a garment that rested upon him, outwardly representing the Spirit of God resting on the prophet's life. When Elijah was taken up to heaven in a whirlwind, his mantle fell to the ground. Elisha picked up the mantle but might have been unsure of what he had until he confronted a problem. He went to the water's edge, struck the water with the garment, and declared, "Where is the God of Elijah?" The waters parted.

## AVOIDING THE BATTLE

Avoiding the battle we were designed for is a mistake none of us can afford. This happened to one of the greatest men ever to live, King David. He was lounging on his rooftop at the time kings were typically fighting a war.

> Then it happened in the spring, at the time when kings go out to battle, that David sent Joab and his servants with him and all Israel, and they destroyed the sons of Ammon and besieged Rabbah. But David stayed at Jerusalem.
>
> Now when evening came David arose from his bed and walked around on the roof of the king's house, and from the roof he saw a woman bathing; and the woman was very beautiful in appearance. So David sent and inquired about the woman. And one said, "Is this not Bathsheba, the daughter of Eliam, the wife of Uriah the Hittite?" David sent messengers and took her, and when she came to him, he lay with her; and when she had purified herself from her uncleanness, she returned to her house.
>
> —2 Samuel 11:1–4

When we refuse to enter the battle we were born for, we expose ourselves to battles we have no grace for. David missed his assignment for battle and fell into sin when he faced something he wasn't prepared to face. This is not to cause paranoia, but it is to bring about the proper fear of the Lord regarding our assignment for advancement. Such promotion for significance is not about us. It is about the full representation of who Jesus is in the earth. That happens whenever we become all He intended.

The safest place for the believer is on the frontlines of battle. I remember hearing this concept many years ago. The cares of the soldier on the front lines are few. They must keep their heads down, make sure they have enough ammunition, and know where their fellow soldiers are. It is simple for sure. But at the back end of the battle, it's a different story. Their concerns are what's for dinner, what movie is showing in the mess hall tent tonight, and when their next leave is. The point is, the simplicity of the frontlines is what makes them the safest place. When our lives get cluttered with too many options, our priorities are prone to become unstable. On the frontlines, we are unsatisfied with any position that does not lead to progress.

## ADVANCING THE KINGDOM

For a believer, the most dangerous place is the place of occupation. It might seem strange, but merely protectively occupying a position that God has given sets us up for an unnecessary threat. Occupation sounds wise. It almost seems noble to safeguard what the Lord has given to us, but it breeds stagnation and *denominationalism*—the forming of regulations and rules to protect previous accomplishments.

Monuments built to past movements are not fluid. They don't adjust with the breath of God that is aimed at His progressive purpose. They are a testimony of what happened in the past, but they don't move with God. And when we don't move with God, we tend to lose what we've gained in the past. Occupying territory in God merely for the purpose of protecting what has happened in the past sets us up for failure. Jesus told His disciples a parable about a guy who received one talent, buried it, and discovered how dangerous a position that was: You end up losing what you have.

I need to state that I'm not at all opposed to denominations. My conflict is with *denominationalism*. Many outside a denomination are more bound by an unhealthy structure than those I know who are free within the religious structure. It's not about the title above the door; it's the structure that restricts the heart to live and demonstrate who Jesus is to this dying world. It's a mindset that we must become free from, regardless of the organizations we have been called to serve. It is critical to remember that the mark of citizenship in this wonderful kingdom is freedom. (See 2 Corinthians 3:17.)

---

When we refuse to enter the battle we were born for, we expose ourselves to battles we have no grace for. *#bornforsignificance*

---

My heart in all of this is to discover how to steward effectively all that God has given us. I want to pass on whatever grace I am walking into my spiritual sons and daughters so that they can take it to another level. Everything has to be expanded. This is a time when accelerated growth needs to be on your mind. It's not an attempt to skip steps, but rather a cry to God: "Give me the grace to learn, to adapt, to shift more quickly than has been possible in the past."

This is not a desire to be a superstar. I want my name known in heaven; I want it known by the powers of darkness. That is all. I want the faithfulness of the Lord to be seen in the people of God to the point that darkness trembles at the mention of our names and heaven rejoices because those who have gone before us know that the price they paid was well worth it, as it set us up for success.

I want to end well. I want all that I pour my life into to end well. Longevity is not just a lesson we learn from the great rulers of empires. There were also kings who started off destructive and cruel, perhaps because of their environment or how they were raised. But, later in life, they repented, and the last leg of their race ended well. There is hope for every single person alive, because God's purpose doesn't go away. We are all in this battle; we are all learning to steward and increase what God has given to us.

---

Monuments built to past movements are not fluid. They don't adjust with the breath of God that is aimed at His progressive purpose. *#bornforsignificance*

---

I long to see the body of Christ enter into a season of accelerated growth and maturity, and then pass that on in a way that the next generation takes what we've given them and advances even further. I want to see that pattern passed through multiple generations, with unending, exponential advancement. David and Solomon experienced this. Solomon is one of the few individuals, perhaps in all of history, who was able to take something that was already glorious and progress it where it had never gone before. I believe that Solomon has a prophetic lesson for us today.

We have to adjust and learn how to receive what was passed on so that we can position ourselves to take it to another level. I realize that later in life, Solomon did stumble, but he began with an absolute conviction to embrace the wisdom of God as the primary focus of his life. So we're going to start with that.

## TURNING WALLS INTO HURDLES

Anytime there has been a move of God, the enemy has tried to put up a wall. However, any time the church has held on to their tenacity in faith, that wall has become a hurdle. And once that hurdle has been surmounted, something powerful has happened. Over and over, throughout the Book of Acts, the church crossed a hurdle, and they suddenly had a powerfully refined focus.

It's amazing how much you can see if you restrict where you're looking. There were hurdles all throughout Acts (see chapters 2, 4, 5, and 6), and the church would refine their focus at every level. Every single time a wall was turned into a hurdle when they passed over it, their focus was immediately refined, resulting in a greater boldness. The same is true today. Any time the people of God refine their focus and are walking in a greater boldness, heaven seems to say, "Amen to that!" And miracles increasingly unfold, revealing a new level of power not previously seen before.

In other words, refining our focus leads to more, and there is always more. No matter how far we go into God's presence and power, there is always more. Wherever we are currently standing is simply a precursor to more. You have been set up and trained; you've tasted of His kingdom, so you can't live another day without possibly getting more. That's the whole point.

When the church of Acts would refine their focus, turn the wall into a hurdle, and experience an increase of boldness bringing a demonstration of extraordinary power, *this would always lead to new measures of fruitfulness.* In Acts 2, the church was being added to daily. Five to ten years after Pentecost, after their faithfulness found them once more pressing into new levels of God, they finally broke into a realm called multiplication. "Then the churches throughout all Judea, Galilee, and Samaria had peace and were edified. And walking in the fear of the Lord and in the comfort of the Holy Spirit, they were multiplied" (Acts 9:31, NKJV). And new believers were multiplied to them.

We never sleepwalk our way into greater demonstrations of power. There has to be boldness somewhere along the line. This doesn't mean we have to shout on street corners. But it does mean that we look the devil in the eye and declare the Word of the Lord. We are to boldly declare what God is saying, putting a demand on the Word of the Lord for the completion of the assignment that God has given us.

## THE EVER-INCREASING KINGDOM

There are many things to live conscious of as we live intentionally in this ever-advancing kingdom. This is the continual increase of revival—the focus of our lives. "Of the increase of His government and peace there will be no end" (Is. 9:7, NKJV). There will be no end to His ever-advancing kingdom. It would be a good practice to drive around your city and think of the systems of the world that are about to belong to King Jesus. There's a particular individual in Redding who has built an economic empire, and, as I drive past his house, I say, "There's a kingdom that is about to belong to Jesus. There's a kingdom."

We don't ever have to be intimidated by sin. If you see a dark story on the news or see something happening in your city that goes against God's teaching, you've just seen a kingdom that is about to belong to Jesus. Refuse to be intimidated by the strategies of the powers of darkness or the measure of past success—it's all temporary. Satan himself has been severed from the source of life; he is a branch that has been cut off and is withering as we speak.

---

We never sleepwalk our way into greater demonstrations of power. There has to be boldness somewhere along the line. *#bornforsignificance*

---

Acts 2:42 says, "And they continued steadfastly in the apostles' doctrine and fellowship, in the breaking of bread, and in prayers" (NKJV). This is most likely two to three years after the day of Pentecost. The Bible's record that "they continued steadfastly," is similar to the way a married couple reaffirms their vows daily by how they speak to and treat each other. It's daily renewing the primary commitment to that individual.

The early church learned this lesson very quickly. The Day of Pentecost was so extraordinary. It had the seed to change all of world history, but that seed had to be tended like all seeds. If they received the life-transforming moment as a gift from God, properly weeded and watered it, that seed would provoke change that would literally shake the course of human history, affecting the course of every nation of the world. But, as glorious and pure as the seed was, without proper tending, even it would die.

> For if the word spoken through angels proved unalterable, and every transgression and disobedience received a just penalty, how will we escape if we neglect so great a salvation? After it was at the first spoken through the Lord, it was confirmed to us by those who heard, God also testifying with them, both by signs and wonders and by

> various miracles and by gifts of the Holy Spirit according to His own will.
>
> —Hebrews 2:2–4

I've been pondering these verses recently. It's a sobering passage because it basically says that we can't just receive revelation from God and then coast on its benefits for the rest of our lives. We have to guard and protect what we have heard from Him.

When we receive a word, we do so knowing that we will never be the same again. But we must reinforce this moment by weeding and watering this garden, giving it a chance to grow. We weed the garden by not allowing contrary ideas to the mind of Christ in our thinking. It is taking thoughts captive as a prisoner until those same thoughts reflect the mind of Christ. (See 2 Corinthians 10:5.) We water the garden by living in worship, continuously conscious of His presence.

I can't make that seed grow, but I can interfere with its development. I can tell you that, through the years of the outpouring of the Holy Spirit in Redding, CA, I have heard many people share their testimony. They were radically touched by God, and they have declared, "I will never be the same again." But many of them forgot to pull their own weeds and stay hydrated in the river of God. Their testimony is the initial evidence of the quality of the seed. It has the unlimited potential of bringing us into a place of destiny, affecting the nations. But, untended—as great as that seed is—it will fail.

---

This is the heart and soul of the generational growth in the Book of Acts: they took things to places never before thought possible because they "continued steadfastly." *#bornforsignificance*

---

We are all in the same boat. We have tremendous desire and vision. Our hunger for more of God and all we've done to pursue Him is like the seedbed of our destiny.

God never sets us up to fail. He never leaves us ill-equipped for our battle. But sometimes He is silent. This is where we need to look back to discover what God has been depositing within us for the last year or so to be reminded that we aren't abandoned. This is the heart and soul of the generational growth in the Book of Acts: they took things to places never before thought possible because they "continued steadfastly." They continually devoted themselves to guarding and protecting the revelation they had received at Pentecost.

## JESUS RECEIVED AND APPREHENDED

These two completely different ways of making progress in the kingdom—receiving or apprehending—emphasize identity and authority, as well as rest and warfare. Jesus illustrated these truths when He announced, "All authority has been given to me…" (Matt. 28:18). The beloved Son of God was honored by His Father, who gave Him all things, including all authority. (See John 13:3 and John 16:15.)

When Jesus ascended to the Father, He brought captives with Him. These were the righteous ones who died before His blood was shed to atone for their sins. After His death, He descended into Sheol, where the dead were held, and took them captive. The righteous were in a place of comfort, also called Abraham's bosom in Luke 16:22.

Paul describes His ascension and descension in his letter to the church at Ephesus.

> When he ascended on high, he took many captives and gave gifts to his people. (What does "he ascended" mean

> except that he also descended to the lower, earthly regions? He who descended is the very one who ascended higher than all the heavens, in order to fill the whole universe.)
>
> —Ephesians 4:8–10, niv

What Jesus received enabled Him to take captive (apprehend) those who were already captives to sin and death. Now they were captives of His freedom. Jesus presented these to the Father as the initial reward of His suffering.

The picture of these two methods for progress being used by Jesus is wonderfully inspiring. He received all from the Father as a Son and then used what He received to take people out of the grip of sin and its consequences.

Most of what you need in life will be brought to you. But most of what you want, you'll have to go and get. This is the wonderful, relational journey we have with our heavenly Father. Using His principles to the fullest is how we enter into the fullness of our significance. The world around us is crying for the very thing you and I were born for. Let's not let them down.

CHAPTER 6

# ADVANCEMENT THROUGH HONOR

We don't always find our significance by receiving, as though we were the focus of the world around us. So much of life in this kingdom is obtained by giving. The fullness of our lives is not measured in what we have. It's measured in what we've given away. And one of the greatest gifts any of us could give is honor. It recognizes God's grace upon a life that people often can't see in themselves. It brings their attention to God, the designer, and to His work of wonder in them—His design.

Giving honor is a transaction of sorts, as it releases the mental, emotional, and spiritual nutrients needed by another human being. It is life. Giving honor to another is one of the most important expressions of God's economy.

---

The fullness of our lives is not measured in what we have. It's measured in what we've given away. *#bornforsignificance*

---

Honor is a necessary supplement to our diet for the inner man. But it's not the meal. The meal comes from the Lord

Himself through what He says about us in His Word. Yet the effect of this transaction of honor from people gives a context for our relationship with God to be measured through human connection.

God said, "It is not good that man should be alone" (Gen. 2:18, NKJV). And while He is talking about marriage, the backdrop is our need for people. We were designed for human connection—not instead of a relationship with God but as a way of measuring the true effect of knowing Him.

Jesus drew our attention to the commandment "Honor your father and your mother." Paul added the reminder that it comes with a promise.

> Children, obey your parents in the Lord, for this is right. Honor your father and mother (which is the first commandment with a promise), so that it may be well with you, and that you may live long on earth.
>
> —Ephesians 6:1–3

There it is. Honor releases life. It's one of the ways God extends favor and life to the believer. Not only does honor release life, but often the measure of honor given is also used to determine the amount of blessing or favor given back.

> But Jesus said to them, "A prophet is not without honor except in his hometown and in his own household." And He did not do many miracles there because of their unbelief.
>
> —Matthew 13:57–58

The absence of honor costs dearly. As we read in Matthew 13, the miracles that were designed for people in Jesus' hometown never happened, as the absence of honor determined what they were able to receive. The Bible goes on to teach that honoring a prophet as a prophet gives us access to the prophet's reward, which basically means it gives us access to the benefit of their ministry. The honor given determines the benefit received. Jesus used this principle in His discourse with His hometown of Nazareth in Luke 4:24–27:

> And He said, "Truly I say to you, no prophet is welcome in his hometown. But I say to you in truth, there were many widows in Israel in the days of Elijah, when the sky was shut up for three years and six months, when a great famine came over all the land; and yet Elijah was sent to none of them, but only to Zarephath, in the land of Sidon, to a woman who was a widow. And there were many lepers in Israel in the time of Elisha the prophet; and none of them was cleansed, but only Naaman the Syrian."

The absence of honor in their culture was the reason they could live within reach of the prophet Elijah, who brought about supernatural supply to the widow at Zarephath, and yet remain in financial need themselves. God took His prophet outside His covenant community to display His heart as a provider. He truly is the perfect Father who delights in being the God of abundance for us all. But Israel missed out entirely.

It wasn't because God wasn't concerned or hadn't made preparations for His people to be cared for. The opposite was true. Provision had been made, but their hands were filled with their own pride, which left no room for God's supply. Pride repels the culture of honor. And honor in the kingdom gives access to the resources of His kingdom.

---

Jesus was sent by the Father to bring freedom, but their hands were full of their own issues, which left no room for God's blessing. *#bornforsignificance*

---

The same can be said of Israel's treatment of Elijah's successor, Elisha. The absence of honor for this prophet caused the people with leprosy to remain diseased. They were not afflicted by God's design; Elisha was God's design. The solution was God's idea. While sickness and disease were present because sin entered the world, he was a prophet anointed by God to release the miracle of healing to Naaman, the general of an enemy army. Once again, God went outside His covenant community to display His heart and nature, all because Israel refused to give the honor needed to provide them with access to healing, the wonderful manifestation of the kingdom of God.

According to Jesus' teaching in Luke 4, the absence of honor was their reason for the lack they experienced as a nation. The absence of honor shaped their own history with God. And now, once again, the people of God, Nazareth, are without what God had intended for them: miracles, which are heaven's answer for human need. Jesus was sent by the Father to bring freedom, but their hands were full of their own issues, which left no room for God's blessing.

## JUSTICE MATTERS

It's not as though God sits up there and says, "If they don't honor me, I won't bless them." God never does or thinks anything out of selfish intent. He only lives out of love, which is His commitment always to do what's best for the person in question.

Simply put, giving honor where it is due is an act of justice. It is making a payment. In the same way we would be faithful with our mortgage payments, so must we be with giving honor.

> Render to all what is due them: tax to whom tax is due; custom to whom custom; fear to whom fear; *honor to*

> *whom honor.* Owe nothing to anyone except to love one another; for he who loves his neighbor has fulfilled the law.
>
> —Romans 13:7–8

Please take notice that honor in this passage is likened unto a debt: something owed. It is a part of our assignment and within our skillset to give honor.

Every person deserves honor for at least two reasons: they are made in the image of God, and God gave them gifts and abilities. It is vital that we see this must include giving honor to people before they come to Christ. The unwillingness of believers to honor an unbeliever says more about us than it does about them.

---

Honoring the Holy Spirit, who has chosen to work through a particular person, is not people worship. It is honoring God to recognize and show value for the one He chooses to work through. *#bornforsignificance*

---

The third reason to give honor is that the Holy Spirit is resting upon them. This is the one missed by Israel in their encounters with Elijah, Elisha, and Jesus. Jesus identified the issue as a hometown problem. In other words, familiarity canceled out their ability to recognize the Spirit of God resting upon someone. Because they failed to recognize the Spirit of God upon them, they missed out on what God had set aside for their sake. Their spiritual blindness caused them to miss the moment when the "kingdom was at hand," or within reach.

Honoring the Holy Spirit, who has chosen to work through a particular person, is not people worship. It is honoring God to recognize and show value for the one He chooses to work through. He takes it personally in the same way He is honored when we give a cup of cold water to someone in need. (See Matthew 25:40.)

## BRINGING PEOPLE TO JESUS

Evangelism has been around for two thousand years. It is vital, as we are facing what will be the greatest harvest of souls the world has ever seen. The harvest is upon us now. But the only reason I mention this subject in the context of honor and promotion is that we are often blind to the tools Jesus used. The proper use of these tools often sets us up for the kind of promotion that He longs for us to receive.

I'm going to mention three that stand out to me and expound on them a bit to give them traction in the context of this chapter.

**1. The bold preaching of the gospel**

I will admit, this is my favorite of all. I love hearing the bold declarations of the gospel of Jesus Christ. The transformation of my life came in large part through the bold preaching of Mario Murillo. He presented a no-compromise gospel: either you're all in or all out. I loved it, and I needed it. If I'm going to select one method to use for the rest of my life, it will be this one. God has honored this method for two thousand years. All the great revivalists were known for this gift. I pray this generation embraces the privilege of being bold in our proclamation of truth.

**2. The blessings of God upon His people**

This will probably seem like the strangest of all evangelistic tools. And I guess it should be, as we've not always known how to carry favor and blessing the way it was designed. And yet the principle remains: blessings upon us reveal Him. And that in part is the purpose of this book. Psalm 67:1–2 addresses this profoundly: "God be merciful to us and bless us, and cause His face to shine upon us. That Your way may be known on earth, Your salvation among all nations" (NKJV). Look at it carefully. God's mercy and blessings displayed upon our lives reveal His nature—"that your way may be known on earth." The next statement is the most astonishing of them all—"Your salvation among the nations." The blessing upon us, carried well, is what reveals the nature of our perfect Father in a way that impacts entire nations. With that outcome hanging in the balance, we might want to give more deliberate attention to this vital tool. I owe the world around me a blessed life because it is that life that reveals His nature in a way that makes His grace irresistible.

**3. Giving honor where it's due**

I doubt this will come as a surprise, but God uses a different standard for seeing where honor is due than we do. In this case, it's not that our perspective is wrong. We know how to recognize nobility and reward accordingly. We also know a bit about recognizing bravery and courage. We rightfully honor our first responders as they face considerable challenges in carrying out their duties. There are many other such things that we are able to recognize and honor.

But Jesus raised the bar on how, when, and to whom we are to give honor. The honor He gave was not according to externals. He honors according to the heart, but also to the potential. Jesus sat next to the offering plate in the synagogue and noticed how some people gave considerable sums of money. But He honored the widow who put in all she had even though her gift was the least. He honored the centurion for his unique understanding of the kingdom in his demonstration of great faith. And so He did with many others, two of which I'll mention next.

## KINDNESS STILL LEADS TO REPENTANCE

Peter (also called Simon) is a favorite character in Scripture for many of us. Perhaps it's because we can so easily identify with his blunders. Toward the beginning of his journey with Jesus, he had an unusual experience while fishing.

> When He had finished speaking, He said to Simon, "Put out into the deep water and let down your nets for a catch." Simon answered and said, "Master, we worked hard all night and caught nothing, but I will do as You say and let down the nets." When they had done this, they enclosed a great quantity of fish, and their nets began to break; so they signaled to their partners in the other boat for them to come and help them. And they came and filled both of the boats, so that they began to sink. But when Simon Peter saw that, he fell down at Jesus' feet, saying, "Go away from me Lord, for I am a sinful man!" For amazement had seized him and all his companions because of the catch of fish which they had taken; and so also were James and John, sons of Zebedee, who were partners with Simon. And Jesus said to Simon, "Do not fear, from now on you will be catching men."
>
> —Luke 5:4–10

Jesus gave direction on where to fish. Peter obeyed and caught more than he could handle, forcing him to call for help from other boats. This miracle caused Peter to drop to his knees in repentance. I remind you that Peter was a fisherman. Catching and selling fish was his business. Jesus gave him such an abundance of fish to sell in his business that he had to share with other businessmen. It was the honor of abundance that brought Peter to repentance. There's no record of Jesus preaching to Peter at this moment. He didn't point out what needed to change. Jesus simply introduced Peter to a kingdom beyond anything he had ever seen or experienced before. And he was willing to forsake all to embrace it.

The final thought for this story is that the extreme abundance of fish would forever be etched into Peter's mind as the standard for the harvest of souls. First is the natural, then the spiritual. (See 1 Corinthians 15:46.) Jesus taught him about abundance in the natural to give him faith and an example of the spiritual fulfillment for which he was born. Natural lessons are extremely important, but it's crucial they don't end there. They are pathways to true spiritual realities and breakthroughs.

When Jesus honored Peter with massive blessing and breakthrough, it might have offended some by stirring up jealousy. But almost everyone would have been offended by the next story. Jesus honored the most dishonorable person in town. The term *tax collector* is synonymous with the word *thief*. And when you add the word *chief* to *tax collector*, you have the most despised person in the whole region. I'm sure the people had a higher opinion of just about everyone, even the more marginal citizens of their community, than the one they perceived as being hired by the government to steal from them.

This is where this story begins. Zacchaeus was very wealthy, most likely at the citizens' expense. When Jesus saw him in the tree observing the events of the day, He invited Himself to Zacchaeus's house for a meal. I'm sure everyone in the crowd would have loved to have Jesus come to their home. But Jesus chose the most despised one to honor in front of everyone. Every time Jesus did something like this, He was revealing that the nature of His world is different from ours.

> When Jesus came to the place, He looked up and said to him, "Zacchaeus, hurry and come down, for today I must stay at your house." And he hurried and came down and

> received Him gladly. When they saw it, they all began to grumble, saying, "He has gone to be the guest of a man who is a sinner." Zacchaeus stopped and said to the Lord, "Behold, Lord, half of my possessions I will give to the poor, and if I have defrauded anyone of anything, I will give back four times as much." And Jesus said to him, "Today salvation has come to this house, because he, too, is a son of Abraham. For the Son of Man has come to seek and to save that which was lost."
>
> —Luke 19:5–10

Jesus honored the thief of all thieves, no doubt stirring up the anger and jealousy of the crowd because He saw the value of this one life. What astonishes me, as one who much prefers the bold preaching of the gospel, is how Jesus didn't speak to the man about his sins. He never instructed him to return the money he took, nor did He tell him to prioritize the poor. And yet, these were evidence of true repentance in this tax collector's heart.

This beautiful response was because Zacchaeus tasted the kindness of Jesus and automatically began to confess and repent. The story ends with this statement, "The Son of Man has come to seek and to save that which was lost." How did Jesus seek this lost soul? Honor. God used honor to draw Zacchaeus into a personal relationship with Him, which connected him to his eternal purpose.

## HONOR IN GIVING

Giving is one of the essential parts of our reason for being. Everything that works in divine order gives, contributes, or serves. The three most basic places from which to give are compassion, vision, and honor.

**1. Compassion**

We give out of compassion when we give to meet human need. If someone has no food, is short on money for rent, or their medical bills are far beyond what they can pay, giving is the compassionate thing to do. To live this way is honorable. The Bible says giving to the poor is lending to the Lord. And He has the best interest rates: thirty, sixty, and hundredfold returns.

**2. Vision**

We give into vision when we tithe and give offerings to our local church, support a missionary, or help our local women's shelter add a new wing to their facility. We are giving because we believe in the vision of that ministry or organization.

**3. Honor**

We give out of honor when we acknowledge the value of someone, and we desire to recognize that person's value with a representative gift. Often there isn't a perceived need. It is basically saying, "Because of who I am in God and who I see you are, I must respond with a gift of honor."

The Queen of Sheba did this and gave an extravagant gift to Solomon, who was the least needy person on the planet. After she spent considerable time with Solomon, he then gave her gifts that were beyond hers in quality and amounts. She wasn't in need, either. She was about to return to her nation and her people, where she had no lack at all. The phrase used in Scripture to describe this act is *royal generosity.* "Now King Solomon gave the queen of Sheba all she desired, whatever she asked, besides what Solomon had given her according to the *royal generosity.* So she turned and went to her own country, she and her servants (I Kings 10:13, NKJV). Giving never diminishes the value of those who know who they are. The opposite is true. The generous become more stable and established.

The gift of honor was illustrated beautifully in the Book of Acts in a most unusual setting: famine.

> Now at this time some prophets came down from Jerusalem to Antioch. One of them named Agabus stood up and began to indicate by the Spirit that there would certainly be a great famine all over the world. And this took place in the reign of Claudius. And in the proportion that any of the disciples had means, each of them determined to send a contribution for the relief of the brethren living in Judea. And this they did, sending it in charge of Barnabas and Saul to the elders.
>
> —Acts 11:27–30

The prophet declared that a famine was coming to the entire world. The response of the people was to take an offering in the face of personal need. That is not normal thinking, at least for this world. And yet, that way of thinking led to an unusual breakthrough. Where was the famine coming to? The whole world. That means that those who took the offering would be affected by the famine, too. And yet they took an offering. That is kingdom thinking.

Where did they give their money? To the brethren in Judea. Were they in need? Perhaps. Is it possible that in the face of crisis, they wanted to send an offering in honor of the people who brought them the gospel in the first place? It's very possible. And while the famine happened, you never hear it spoken of again. A gift of honor silenced even the voice of a famine.

The power of honor is truly transformational. We don't get the benefits of one kingdom by following the laws of another.

Offerings, especially ones of honor, pull the heart and mind away from all that is inferior.

They honored those who brought the good news, joining with Isaiah's decree.

> How lovely on the mountains are the feet of him who brings good news, who announces peace and brings good news of happiness, who announces salvation, and says to Zion, "Your God reigns!"
>
> —Isaiah 52:7

Never is it foolish to honor the one God honors and celebrate the one God celebrates. Yes, it is true He celebrates us all, but there are times when it is wisdom to recognize where God has put His attention in a given moment. Responding to His lead is always healthy. And He rewards those who follow His heart for others.

Several individuals are a large part of my history in God. Their influence and selfless investment in me have changed my life forever. I always try to take advantage of the opportunities to honor them with giving.

We do this as a church family, too. It is common to give offerings to ministries after they've ministered to you. It's the right thing to do. But we have supported older saints who ministered faithfully to us in their prime, who, because of their health or age, were unable to travel anymore. We choose to give in honor to the ones we could no longer benefit from. In one case, we continued our financial support for the wife after her husband went home to be with the Lord. This, of course, is offered in thanks to God, who blessed them that they might be a blessing to us.

## RELEASING FAVOR

One of the most unusual principles I've seen in Scripture is that we have the ability to increase the favor or grace upon another person's life. This is the process of stewarding the favor on our lives for the benefit of another. This is a fantastic example of using favor to benefit another. But the way it works is quite amazing.

> Let no unwholesome word proceed from your mouth, but only such a word as is good for edification according to the need of the moment, so that it will give grace to those who hear.
>
> —Ephesians 4:29

Just find words that edify according to the need of the moment because they will give grace to those who hear. Grace is undeserved favor that enables them to come into their destiny and live as Jesus did.

Grace is correctly defined as unmerited favor. But that is only the beginning. It is favor that enables. I like to put it this way: The Law requires, but grace enables. It enables us to do what only Jesus could do.

I would never want to imply that we direct God's hand or in some way control Him. That would be the ultimate foolishness. Yet truth often gets close to the error we fear the most. When we live in reaction to error instead of response to the truth, we miss what God is saying and create another error in the process. In this case, God is saying that when I come to my brother and speak encouraging words to him, I am saying, "God, because of the favor you have put on my life, I ask that you impart the same favor to my brother."

We steward the favor of God when we choose to encourage, bless, and minister to someone. Grace is from God, but when we take the posture of being a strength to someone else through speaking words of encouragement, we are marking people for an increase of divine favor. Amazing! God favors the one I favor. This is a beautiful picture of co-laboring with the Lord.

It would be wrong to imply that an individual didn't have favor before I came along. Each is given a measure. But I remind you again even Jesus needed to increase in favor with God and man. That being saidwe could all use more. Everyone should welcome the increase we bring.

I like to picture it this way: my words mark someone's life with a bull's-eye, asking God to strike the mark with blessing and increase. This is being a steward of God's grace through a generous heart. Many are generous with money, especially if they have much, but fail miserably with a generous heart in looking to strengthen others through kindness. This is real generosity.

I would never want to imply that we can twist God's arm or in some way control or force Him to do anything. He is sovereign. You and I are not. But He has written our role into His sovereign plan, and delights in our involvement in the unfolding of His plan of grace for others. To illustrate this concept, a prophet friend once told me, "If you know of a church where you think I need to go, tell me, and I'll go there." He wasn't in need of another meeting; he was highly respected all over the world. What did he mean, then? In so many words, he was saying, "Bill, you have favor in my eyes, and if somebody has favor in your eyes, I'll show them the same kindness I've shown you." I find it interesting that he modeled the Lord's heart revealed in the Ephesians 4 passage quite well. It is the way of the kingdom.

The Lord makes it clear as to what kinds of things need to be said. "Let no unwholesome words proceed from your mouth."

He then directs us to speak words that build up according to the need of the moment. God's assignment for us is to give encouragement to people. In a very real sense, we open up opportunities for God to increase His blessings on that person. Because we choose them, God chooses them."

## HONORING THE PRE-BELIEVER

As I mentioned earlier, I don't wait for people to get saved to give them honor. I know the concern is for us not to insulate people from their awareness of their own sin. After all, there's no need for a savior without the awareness of our lost condition. In the conviction of sin, we find the open door to turn from sin with faith toward God. Yet I've found that most people live aware of what is wrong in their lives. Few people live with an awareness of how God values them. I believe that the Lord is bringing people to a place of great tenderness because of honor. We have already seen it.

I have practiced this principle for decades. Years ago, I wrote a letter to a judge who had made a decision in a court case the opposite of what we were hoping for. It concerned a new convert whose life turned around because of Jesus. The judge sought for justice while I sought for mercy. When the case was over, I wrote the judge a letter, thanking him for his passion for justice for our city. We need it. He wrote back, saying, "We don't get letters like this." It's good to give honor to people for carrying out their position responsibly in our city.

---

Few people live with an awareness of how God values them. I believe that the Lord is bringing people to a place of great tenderness because of honor. *#bornforsignificance*

---

I remember a businessman who was enduring a lot of opposition because of some apartments he was building. Our small town had a great lack of places to live. And those apartments were a beautiful addition to our city. One day I stood in his place of business, hearing him take verbal abuse for his building project. There's a very unhealthy approach to business and businesspeople that is working to kill ingenuity and hoping to make the concept of profits immoral. It is demonic in nature, as it is working to undermine what makes communities healthy. Of course, illegal gains, or profits from immorality, are wrong. But by nature, profits reinforce to a culture the concept of sowing and reaping.

When Jesus taught on this subject, He spoke of talents and minas, both of which were sums of money. The smallest amount of profit illustrated in His story was one hundred percent profit. He then took from the one who had the least, the one who refused to use what was given him in a responsible way, and gave it to the one who had the most. That destroys anyone's chance of making Jesus a communist or socialist leader. He was not even close. His compassion for hurting humanity did not cancel His wisdom for what makes a community healthy. We must recover the value of both healthy, profit-making businesses and compassion for those who have suffered unjustly. Businesses that offer services and make a profit are beneficial for all of us.

After hearing him suffer such abuse, I went home and wrote him a letter, thanking him for taking his profits in business and investing them back into our city. The whole city benefited from the much-needed housing and the excellence with which he was building. He thanked me later for my kindness.

Honoring people is a great privilege we have in life. It reveals our own healthy outlook that is neither self-absorbed nor merely church-absorbed. Many who are generous in church settings are mean and stingy outside of that context. This must change. Looking at people with respect and honor goes a long way in helping our cities reach their potential and positions us for increase and promotion.

Our significance is not measured in what we've received from others. We are designed for generosity. Our role is to draw from the King's resources and share them with as many people as possible. This is more than material. It is the complete realm of God's kingdom. Our lives are to inspire people into greater manifestations of righteousness, peace, and joy in their individual lives. This is His intended purpose for us all.This is where my own significance is found.

CHAPTER 7

# LOYALTY, THE SECRET TOOL FOR ADVANCEMENT

I HAD THE PRIVILEGE of serving under my dad's leadership for five years. We had a wonderful staff. They all seemed to think outside the box quite easily. It was fun, and my dad was so accommodating and supportive. His ability to stand alongside younger men and women was quite legendary. I still see people today that had my dad in their corner when others in leadership positions had passed them by. He modeled loyalty at a high level and showed us what it looked like to give grace to the underdog.

I'll never forget the conversation he had with all of us on his pastoral staff one day. He sat us down to share his values. He told us that if we ever had a problem with alcohol, he'd work with us. He then went on to mention several other sins that people fall into. But he concluded his list with this statement: "But if you are ever disloyal, you are out of here."

The heart of God became very apparent at that moment. He was letting us know that behavior can be worked on. But heart is everything. And if the heart is wrong, you're gone.

Loyalty is a fascinating subject, especially if we look at it from God's perspective as described in Proverbs 20:6: "Many a man proclaims his own loyalty, but who can find a trustworthy man?" This verse is quite alarming to me. It is basically saying, "All think they are loyal. But I disagree." I don't think God is saying that no one is loyal. We have beautiful examples of it in Scripture. But what concerns me is that God implies that our perspective of loyalty is not the same as His. Let's face it. My opinion of myself has no value whatsoever if it is in conflict with what God says. He is right, and everyone else is to be found a liar. I have set my interests fully toward His opinion on everything. It's the only way to live responsibly and successfully.

---

My opinion of myself has no value whatsoever if it is in conflict with what God says. *#bornforsignificance*

---

He likens loyalty to being trustworthy. Anyone can be found trustworthy when things are going well. But our dependability is challenged during conflict and trial. That is where God measures our trustworthiness. The word *trustworthy* can be translated "faithful," and in at least one case, "messenger of faithfulness."

This is no small subject for me. "Great Is Thy Faithfulness" is probably my favorite hymn of all time. It moves me to tears. And what I value most about Him, He values about us. He constantly looks for people who carry His nature of faithfulness, that they might more accurately represent Him, regardless of circumstances. The world deserves a witness of His character through greatness, faithfulness, and kindness. We are the messengers of these things.

This is deeply connected to our significance because without character the subject of significance can only become an egocentric journey that takes us deeper in pride and independence.

Such things are valued by the world around us, but seriously compromise our purpose in this life and beyond.

## REBELLION CONSIDERED A VIRTUE

Today's society is working hard to redefine everything about life, saying right is wrong and wrong is right. The boundaries for reasonable thinking have been removed so far that what was considered insanity only a few years ago is today called logic, reason, and mercy. This is happening on *our watch*. Protest banners aren't the answer. Right living, in the open, works. Our lives are like leaven. Once the leaven is worked into the dough (society), it cannot be removed. It reestablishes our "spiritual due north," providing the biblical plumb line to culture once again.

My generation exalted rebellion as a way of life. *Question Authority* became the bumper sticker that represented a way of thinking. And while there has always been abuse of authority, one wrong doesn't justify another equally destructive wrong. Jesus didn't react to the devil. He responded to the Father. Hating a lie doesn't remove the power of the lie. Only truth can do that. Truth more than makes up for the effects of a lie.

Rebellion can get a person recognition and even promotion in some settings if the organization is broken. It will be called something noble to justify it, and it will work in some environments. But not with God. He gives promotion according to our hearts. And His promotion comes with no sorrow. "It is the blessing of the Lord that makes rich, and He adds no sorrow to it." (Prov. 10:22). And while this verse deals with money, the broader subject of wealth includes position, promotion, and money. The point is, He protects what He blesses.

## A MOST UNUSUAL TEACHER

I doubt there was a Jew alive in Jesus' day who thought one of the great lessons of the kingdom of God would come from a soldier, but it did. And it was profound, in that it carried unusual understanding of authority and faith. It ended in an extraordinary miracle. But the process is unique in that it illustrates a fundamental truth: the way you operate under leadership gives you the authority to operate in leadership. This is the way of promotion.

> And when Jesus entered Capernaum, a centurion came to Him, imploring Him, and saying, "Lord, my servant is lying paralyzed at home, fearfully tormented." Jesus said to him, "I will come and heal him." But the centurion said, "Lord, I am not worthy for You to come under my roof, but just say the word, and my servant will be healed. For I also am a man under authority, with soldiers under me; and I say to this one, 'Go!' and he goes, and to another, 'Come!' and he comes, and to my slave, 'Do this!' and he does it." Now when Jesus heard this, He marveled and said to those who were following, "Truly I say to you, I have not found such great faith with anyone in Israel..." And Jesus said to the centurion, "Go; it shall be done for you as you have believed." And the servant was healed that very moment.
>
> —Matthew 8:5–10, 13

This story carries one of the great principles of promotion in the Bible. Here we have a centurion who understands the structures and responsibilities found in all authority. He reasoned that Jesus must be in right relationship with the Father because of what He demonstrated in His life. He spoke, and things happened. Israel missed this profound lesson. This soldier revealed his understanding when he told Jesus that all He had to do was give a command, because he, as a centurion, was also under authority.

---

Hating a lie doesn't remove the power of the lie.
Only truth can do that. *#bornforsignificance*

---

You would think if he were going to applaud Jesus' authority, he would have said, "I, too, am a man *of* authority. I tell people what to do, and they do it." Instead, he says that he also is a man *under* authority, and "I say to this one, 'Go,' and he goes and to this one 'come' and he comes." He acknowledges that Jesus represents the Father, but he also reveals that using our positions (places of promotion) well is according to how well we represent those over us.

## A DIRTY WORD

*Submission* has almost become a dirty word to some. Scripture is often twisted to make it say anything but what it is saying, often going to the other extreme—in this case, making rebellion a noble act. Once again, the abuse of this subject by many has ruined this rich truth for a large part of a generation. Yet the reality of truth remains the same. Submission is God's way to promotion and increase. I like to put it this way to our teams: "When you submit to someone, you don't always get to do what you want. But you do get to do more than you're capable of doing." Submission has that effect. It gives us access to another person's strength until that strength becomes our own. Let me illustrate.

When I left the position of being an associate pastor under my dad's leadership, I became a senior pastor at Mountain Chapel in Weaverville, California. But I would only accept that position under the agreement with the church board that I could meet regularly with my dad and submit our work to him for input and direction. He was the perfect guy to submit to as he only had our interest in mind and had no personal agenda whatsoever. I had never been a senior pastor before. This automatically gave me twenty-five years of experience. His history became mine.

---

When you submit to someone, you don't always get to do what you want. But you do get to do more than you're capable of doing. *#bornforsignificance*

---

I don't think loyalty is possible without the practice of biblical submission. There is no leadership without authority. Even responsibility has its roots in authority. The effect we have on people is to the degree that we have responded to the authority over us. Our capacity for living in promotion well is according to this vital virtue.

Many don't realize this as they aspire to new positions of leadership, to new places of service in the body of Christ, or even the community. But because they have not dealt with their underlying attitudes and issues toward authority, they don't realize that God keeps pressing them down and will not give them the promotion. Rebellion is poison. And it will creep up in a given situation and infect many. For this reason, God withholds the promotion He has for a person until they are reduced to their place of strength, which is anchored in submission.

## LOYALTY TO AN UNGODLY KING

Daniel's story is remarkable for many reasons. One that should be celebrated by us all is that he remained faithful throughout his long life, representing God well and serving in challenging situations without compromise. His really is one of the more beautiful stories in the Bible. So many fail in the final moments of their lives and don't finish strong as God intended. I don't want to be one who does well for a season but falters when the pressure increases. Daniel is the prototype of a faithful leader. He managed his promotion well.

He was somewhere around fifteen years old when he was removed from his family and taken to Babylon to serve King Nebuchadnezzar. Oftentimes, the other family members were killed when one was taken in this manner. Daniel's name was changed to the name of Nebuchadnezzar's god, Belteshazzar. Daniel and his three friends, Shadrach, Meshach, and Abednego, were trained in the ways of Babylon.

It is also quite possible they were made eunuchs. The Hebrew word for *eunuch* is *saris*. *Saris* is also translated as governmental official. But that interpretation would have no punch when it was used in Isaiah's rebuke of Hezekiah. He said some of his sons would be taken captive and made *saris*. It would mean little if it meant they would be made "governmental officials." It is likely that these Hebrew boys were made eunuchs. I only make this point to emphasize the issues of the heart that they had to walk through to be successful in the Babylonian system. This makes this story all the more moving. And though their positions of influence are a promotion from God's perspective, I'm sure it didn't seem that way at first for these four.

They were immersed in a devilish system, filled with witchcraft and sorcery. Their entire world was filled with the demonic. King Nebuchadnezzar even made an idol in his image and then attempted to kill anyone who didn't bow down in worship. This is where we get the wonderful story of the three Hebrew children in the fiery furnace. (See Daniel 3.) Daniel was considered the chief of the magicians, which basically means the king thought him to be another occultist. And yet Daniel thrived in this environment, unoffended, so much so he stood out head and shoulders above the rest. He was considered the wise one, who gained a reputation for interpreting dreams and giving wise counsel, in whom lived the "spirit of the holy gods" (Dan. 4:9). I chuckle a bit when I hear people describe how dark their work environment is. Daniel set the highwater mark for living in a dark environment and thriving.

There are so many reasons this prophet should have failed in his service to the king or, at a minimum, walked with a spiritual limp for the rest of his life. Yet he stood tall in his love and service for God and his loyalty to the king. While much about this story is worthy of study, this is all we need for this particular lesson.

## DEFENDING THE UNGODLY

Defending the ungodly is not the same as defending ungodliness. This became apparent in one of my favorite stories in the Bible pertaining to loyalty. This virtue in this prophet was about to transform the worst of the worst kings ever.

Daniel had interpreted a dream for Nebuchadnezzar in a most bizarre way, telling the king both the dream and the interpretation. When Daniel did this, he saved the lives of all the other magicians in the process. (See Daniel 2.) It's interesting how God will use the righteousness of one of His servants to preserve the lives of those who would otherwise be lost. He did this with the apostle Paul in the story of his shipwreck. God spared Paul's life as well as that of everyone else on the ship, just to keep His apostle alive for a witness in Rome. (See

Acts 27:22.) It's an important biblical reality that many benefit from the effect of one righteous life. Living for God releases His favor to those under our influence. This is the wonderful grace of God.

Nebuchadnezzar then had a second dream and wanted an interpretation. Of course, he went to Daniel after the magicians, conjurers, and diviners couldn't interpret the dream. He paid him one of the highest compliments ever, saying, "no mystery baffles you" (Dan. 4:9). The New King James Version puts it, "no secret *troubles* you." Wouldn't it be good for the rulers of this world to look to the church and say, "You don't seem to be troubled by the things you don't understand." Such is the lifestyle of hope.

Here is the story: In the first part of the dream, the king saw a large tree that was visible to the whole earth. It was glorious and wonderful but was eventually chopped down. It was a message concerning the greatness of the king that would be brought to nothing. After seven years, he would be restored, emphasizing God's ability to raise up and cast down.

> Then Daniel, whose name is Belteshazzar, was appalled for a while as his thoughts alarmed him. The king responded and said, "Belteshazzar, do not let the dream or its interpretation alarm you." Belteshazzar replied, "My lord, if only the dream applied to those who hate you and its interpretation to your adversaries!"
>
> —Daniel 4:19

Here's what brings me to tears in this story. Daniel is a righteous prophet without compromise. Yet he was genuinely grieved when his assignment, King Nebuchadnezzar, was about to be judged by God according to the interpretation of his dream. Daniel said, "If only the dream applied to those who hate you and its interpretation to your adversaries." This is stunning. Most leaders I know of would have stated to this king, "I told you so! You can't live the way you live and not expect the judgment of God on your life. I'm only surprised it didn't happen sooner." But not Daniel. He was sincerely saddened by the news. He then gave counsel that possibly the king would be spared this calamity or, at a minimum, have it delayed. He seemed to really love the man he was assigned to serve.

---

Love does not rejoice in wrong suffered by anyone...God alone has the right for vengeance. We don't. *#bornforsignificance*

---

How do you live with this kind of loyalty? I can see people displaying this kind of loyalty if they worked for Mother Theresa. But not with this king. Here's the clincher: Daniel is one of the most righteous prophets ever, serving the most wicked king ever. But instead of "I told you so," we hear genuine grief for his sentence from God. He walked a tightrope in that he was grieved over the king's pending punishment, but was not offended with God for handing out such a decree.

## THE PRIESTLY ROLE

Love does not rejoice in wrong suffered by anyone. There is a loyalty that needs to be demonstrated with compassion and love for people. God alone has the right for vengeance. We don't. And when we accuse the unrighteous, we are misusing our priestly responsibility. (Every believer is a priest unto the Lord, according to 1 Pet. 2:9.) I once had a woman rebuke me and try to cast a demon out of me at the end of a Sunday morning service when I refused to curse the city of San Francisco with her. She was exhibiting the wrong use of authority.

If I misuse my authority, God will defend the one I've attacked. But if I use my priestly role to intercede for and love the person who is wrong, God will discipline them simply because they have the support needed to endure. This is an interesting principle in Scripture that I first heard about around thirty years ago. This beautiful combination often culminates in the transformation of the one under God's correction. To lovingly support must not work against God's dealings. Instead, we patiently love in spite of their circumstances.

Daniel lived faithfully in his assignment. And while there wasn't a positional promotion for him, as he was already at the top in his role, he was able to serve four different kings, each with the same result: righteousness prevailed. The end result of Nebuchadnezzar's story is his complete repentance. Consider this point: the vilest of leaders was transformed through the loyalty of one righteous man.

## CHILDREN NEED EXAMPLES

Daniel had something powerful in his heart; it was a love and passion for his leader. This kind of heart would change the climate of business and education in our cities, and even our nations. Simply guarding the lips and the comments that are made about our public leaders would have a tremendous effect on our homes and the priestly destinies of the next generation. Parents can't be careless in their speech about their bosses, pastors, presidents, and other leaders, and think their children will be unaffected. Remember the principle of reaping and sowing. For me to speak evil of a leader makes me an open target as a leader in my home. It's reaping and sowing.

Parents, I want to encourage you on this subject. We have to work hard as parents to teach the principles of respect, and your children are going to check it out by your conversation and how you act. Do you roll your eyes when a certain person goes by? It's vital to set a good example because it prepares them for their own promotion and places of ever-increasing influence throughout their lives. Their approach to others in leadership will affect their own destinies.

I will tell you where the rub comes. I can't believe how many parents believe their children's far-out stories of how horrible their teacher is and how righteous their kids are. When our kids went to the public high school, they got into some hard situations with some poor teachers, but we would talk about how we had prayed before we sent them to school and how God must have wanted that teacher for them. God was working to cultivate depth of character in them. If something immoral or opposed to principles of life came their way, we would draw the line and come to defend. But we did not jump into every squabble to make sure that our Johnny was protected. The reason we didn't is that I wanted them to understand that pressures come to them for reasons unseen. God is big enough to use whatever we face for His glory and our strength.

---

It's vital to set a good example because it prepares [children] for their own promotion and places of ever-increasing influence throughout their lives. *#bornforsignificance*

---

## THE SCHOOL OF KINGS

Before David ever became king, he served Saul for a season. And while I've dealt with this in measure elsewhere in the book, here is a refresher with more information. David's success made Saul jealous. Don't think that promotion will always make everyone around you happy. It doesn't. Mary, the mother of Jesus, was highly favored of the Lord. But not even her husband-to-be believed her story. She was highly favored—and highly opposed. Sometimes, that's the way it works.

David's school of training for reigning involved many strange situations. During this decade-plus of running from Saul, the king had a couple of opportunities to kill him. Interestingly, his men prophesied to him that this was God's will and David's chance to step into his appointed destiny. Here is yet another glance at biblical promotion from God's perspective. Saul pursued David, who was hiding in a cave.

> He came to the sheepfolds on the way, where there was a cave; and Saul went in to relieve himself. Now David and his men were sitting in the inner recesses of the cave. The men of David said to him, "Behold, this is the day of which the LORD said to you, 'Behold; I am about to give your enemy into your hand, and you shall do to him as it seems good to you.'" Then *David arose and cut off the edge of Saul's robe* secretly. It came about afterward that *David's conscience bothered him* because he had cut off the edge of Saul's robe. So he said to his men, "Far be it from me because of the LORD that I should do this thing to my lord, the LORD's anointed, to stretch out my hand against him, since he is the LORD's anointed."
>
> —1 SAMUEL 24:3–6

David defaced the appearance of his lord, King Saul. His conscience bothered him because of such a thing. I wonder how often believers cut off the corner of the robe of the reputation of their leaders. And this is usually done to good men and women, not a king like Saul, who was a demonized man who had turned from following the Lord.

> David persuaded his men with these words and did not allow them to rise up against Saul. And Saul arose, left the cave, and went on his way. Now afterward David arose and went out of the cave and called after Saul, saying, "My lord the king!" And when Saul looked behind him, David bowed with his face to the ground and prostrated himself. David said to Saul, "Why do you listen to the words of men, saying, 'Behold, David seeks to harm you'? Behold, this day your eyes have seen that the Lord had given you today into my hand in the cave, and some said to kill you, but my eye had pity on you; and I said, 'I will not stretch out my hand against my lord, for he is the Lord's anointed.' Now, my father, see! Indeed, see the edge of your robe in my hand! For in that I cut off the edge of your robe and did not kill you, know and perceive that there is no evil or rebellion in my hands, and I have not sinned against you, though you are lying in wait for my life to take it."
>
> — 1 Samuel 24:7–11

David humbled himself before the king and his army. Though there may have been some distance between them, they were close enough to talk. Face to the ground is a very vulnerable position of humility, not a position of strength. I believe this to be a position of sincere confession and repentance. Had David killed him, he would have become king. God had already set him up for that. The only question that remained was, What kind of king would he be, and how long would his throne last?

> May the LORD judge between you and me, and may the LORD avenge me on you; but my hand shall not be against you. As the proverb of the ancients says, "Out of the wicked comes forth wickedness"; but my hand shall not be against you. After whom has the king of Israel come out? Whom are you pursuing? A dead dog, a single flea? The LORD therefore be judge and decide between you and me; and may He see and plead my cause and deliver me from your hand.
>
> —1 SAMUEL 24:12–15

---

Don't think that promotion will always make everyone around you happy. It doesn't. *#bornforsignificance*

---

David understood the judgments of the Lord and that Saul had forsaken the Lord. But he also understood that he could not obtain his rightful position of king over Israel through self-promotion. The throne must be given to him by God Himself, not be obtained as the result of his own finagling.

> When David had finished speaking these words to Saul, Saul said, "Is this your voice, my son David?" Then Saul lifted up his voice and wept. He said to David, "You are more righteous than I; for you have dealt well with me, while I have dealt wickedly with you. You have declared today that you have done good to me, that the LORD delivered me into your hand and yet you did not kill me. For if a man finds his enemy, will he let him go away safely? May the LORD therefore reward you with good in return for what you have done to me this day. Now, behold, I know that you will surely be king, and that the

> kingdom of Israel will be established in your hand. So now swear to me by the Lord that you will not cut off my descendants after me and that you will not destroy my name from my father's household." David swore to Saul. And Saul went to his home, but David and his men went up to the stronghold.
>
> —1 Samuel 24:16–22

David remained loyal in this most difficult situation. Saul came face to face with his own evil, as well as face to face with David's integrity. He was overwhelmed by David's kindness and devotion. And while we have no record of Saul's full repentance, he did acknowledge that David was fit for the position.

He asked for his descendants to be protected, which David did for Mephibosheth and his family. Saul admitted that David would be king instead of his own son Jonathan, who would have been the rightful heir. Interestingly, Jonathan also knew this and had encouraged David to this end. Tragically, Jonathan's life was cut short, fighting alongside his father, Saul. Jonathan would be a fascinating study in loyalty, as he stood with his father, but lived in tender friendship with David.

If there were ever situations where it would have been difficult to be loyal to authority, these two stories fit the bill. First, we see Daniel and his extraordinary heart of loyalty to an evil king, followed by David and his heart of loyalty to Saul, who was another very broken leader. Their examples to us were very pure.

David's situation was at a time when taking the life of a perceived enemy seemed quite natural and easy. Yet David's heart smote him because he had tarnished the image of his leader. One thing we have to remember is the way we treat other people is the way God thinks we have treated Him. He says in Matthew 25:40, "To the extent that you did it to one of these brothers of Mine, even the least of them, you did it to Me." When Stephen was stoned to death, and God later confronted Paul before his conversion, he asked, "Why are you persecuting Me?" (Acts 9:4). And when you unveil the nakedness of a person, Jesus says, "You've done it to Me." The same when you slander and criticize.

## LOYALTY IN THE FAMILY OF GOD

Unlike David, Christians every day deface someone in authority. They blemish or tarnish the image of that person to someone else. I remember teaching these principles in Weaverville over a number of years. A gentleman who was a part of our church family once owned a major Christian publishing company. At one time, he did research on people and kept files on the sins of major Christian leaders. I don't believe he did it with evil intent. Like many, he wanted the church to be holy. I remember through the years trying to minister on the subject. I knew we had a breakthrough when my friend came to me and said, "I took all my files, and I've destroyed them." This was years and years of work.

---

While I don't think it's proper to ignore problems, it's also not everyone's business to fix every problem. *#bornforsignificance*

---

Here's a story I'll paraphrase from Genesis 9. Noah was drunk, naked, and lying on his bed. One of his sons saw it, and he went to get his brother and said, "Dad is drunk. He's naked. Come and look. You won't believe it." The other son refused to do it but came into the room backward with a blanket. He refused to look at his father's nakedness and made sure his dad was covered before he would turn and look.

While I don't think it's proper to ignore problems, it's also not everyone's business to fix every problem. Pray. Love. Support those who have to get into the fray and sort through things into a place of healing and restoration.

If you were around during the eighties, you likely remember the moral failure of a number of well-known ministry leaders. It captured national media attention and I remember one news network decided to have a panel discussion with Christian leaders who had maintained respect through their humility and godly behavior. I'll never forget the comment made by the news network's host. "When we do a news story, it takes a lot of research. We have to call and do a lot of digging to get information. It takes us a long time to do the research to get a good story. But with these scandals, you guys called us." It felt like a gut punch. The church had turned on itself. And we did so in front of the world, to our shame.

It's interesting that many diseases that have risen to the forefront are those where the human body turns against itself. Maybe we have given disease permission to mirror the condition of the church.

## HEALTHY LEADERS

Promotion is about an increase of influence and responsibility. It is always about leadership. And leadership is an issue of the heart. God is concerned about the character of a leader, and that is where He puts the anointing. We all can only go as far as we can be entrusted with authority.

This concept was so radical in the New Testament that Paul put it this way, "Be subject to one another in the fear of Christ"

(Eph. 5:21). In other words, honor the next person you see with your humble heart of submission in the same way you would Jesus. Developing His value system positions us for significance. It's what positions us to fulfill our purpose in life: to be blessed that we might be a blessing.

## CHAPTER 8

# ADVERSE WINDS INVITE

My parents used to live in Santa Cruz, California. Every year our family would take seven to ten days of our vacation and spend it in that oceanside community. We always stayed with my mom and dad, referring to their home as the Johnson Hilton. They loved to have us there and made sure we ate well. These are some of our greatest family memories.

That part of California has hot sun coupled with cool ocean breezes. I always loved that combination. Our family has a special love for the ocean. We love the various parts of ocean life as well: the harbors, piers, and beaches. We spent many days enjoying this part of our beautiful state.

Vacationing year after year in the same place gave us the chance to develop traditional family outings. Besides the hours on the beach and the boardwalk, we loved going out to eat. One of our favorite restaurants was called the Crow's Nest. It was on the beach—or should I say more accurately, *in* the beach. The sand came up to the windows. It was located a stone's throw from the water, as well as next to a harbor filled with boats. Wednesday night was our favorite night to eat at this restaurant because the sailboat regatta took place that night. Dozens and dozens of sailboats would file past our window to enter the sea for this gala. It was a brilliant sight to see the beautiful sails and admirable skills employed by those who sailed the boats.

## FASCINATIONS AND LOGIC

I admit I'm not a sailor. I've only been sailing twice in my life. Once was with very peaceful and calm breezes on a lake. It was the kind of sailing that could inspire one to write a classical music piece. The second time was quite different. It was in the ocean by Santa Cruz with a good friend. It was fun, but also very sobering, especially when you don't know what you're doing. I enjoyed it, but I was also very glad to get back to the dock.

On that second excursion, I began to learn one of the most counterintuitive things I have ever heard: you can sail a boat into the wind. I know that it only appears illogical to one who is ignorant of the laws of sailing. You can sail against the wind. Amazing.

---

Sometimes you can tell where you're supposed to go in life by recognizing where the opposition is coming from. *#bornforsignificance*

---

I love how God created things to be explored. Curiosity and fascination invite us to discover the laws of His creation. I wonder who the first sailor was that discovered if they managed their sail and rudder correctly, they could go where the wind didn't seem to want them to go. There's a spiritual parallel to this: oftentimes our destinies are on the other side of adverse winds.

My friend and associate, Kris Vallotton, puts it this way, "The dogs of doom bark at the doors of your destiny." It might seem strange to look at it this way, but sometimes you can tell where you're supposed to go in life by recognizing where the opposition is coming from. I think the enemy fears our becoming all that God intended us to be, and he hopes that adversity will keep us from pursuing our purpose more fully.

The nautical term for this phenomenon is called *tacking*. With the proper use of the sail and the rudder, one can sail into the wind. Think about it. We can advance against the prevailing winds into the places we long to go. To my way of thinking, the sail is the attitude of the heart, and the rudder is our tongue. Managing my heart and confession goes a long way in ensuring I enter my purpose, or my significance, more completely.

## STUMBLING BLOCKS OR STEPPING-STONES

Each of us must face hard experiences in life. They are common but unpleasant. Some of them are severe and painful, and others are just annoying. Either way, each provides us the opportunity to grow. These are the places where you either stumble or advance. The circumstance doesn't determine the outcome. You do. The position of your heart before God is what determines whether your problem is a place to fall or a stepping-stone into His designed future.

Navigating tough times is hardest when we lose sight of His goodness and faithfulness. He is our trust, our confidence, and our glory. He is the one who has promised us that He will cause all things to work to our good and His glory. In the same way that not every ingredient in a recipe tastes good, so not every part of our lives is enjoyed. Yet the master chef is able to take the things we dislike completely and help them to fit into the overall recipe of a life that testifies of His goodness and grace. Tough things also reveal who we belong to.

---

The position of your heart before God is what determines whether or not your problem is a place to fall or a stepping-stone into His designed future. *#bornforsignificance*

---

The growth from these experiences is what prepares you for significance, for promotion, and for receiving your inheritance. Every challenging experience is an invitation to your future. Here are some that are common to all:

**Disappointment**

If I don't know how to handle disappointment well, I cannot be trusted with the fulfilled dreams God longs for me to experience. It's a challenging test. Many have lost their capacity to dream because of the effect of disappointment on their hearts. It just seemed easier not to dream than to face disappointment again. And yet we owe Him the heart that can dream.

This hurdle is necessary for those who long for the significance they were born for, as the weight of answered prayers becomes too glorious to handle in that weak condition of the heart. Strength of heart is measured in our surrender to His grace working in us.

When the heart is pure and courageous, the ability to dream remains strong. Opposition strengthens our resolve to fulfill our purpose. We were designed to dream and dream big. Such is the process of promotion. And such is the discovery of our position of being co-laborers with God.

**Loss**

If I cannot handle loss in a redemptive way, I cannot be trusted with the gain God has purposed for my life. Maintaining trust in our Father, who always has the last say, is vital to navigating these moments.

Loss is a seed that falls into the ground and dies. We must not waste our losses, as each of them has the potential of bringing forth fruit to His glory and our strength. If I waste my losses through bitterness, anger, and withdrawal, I will have wasted the most precious part of my life in Christ: the death of a dream that leads to a resurrection. If we plant our losses into the care of a loving Father, He, in turn, causes them to bring forth fruit on a scale that we could never bring about on our own. Giving thanks in the midst of these trials is part of what keeps me conscious of His loving care.

While I may be unstable in seasons, He is the rock. Returning to His uncompromising goodness is the ultimate safe place from which to address any problem. Understanding that no issue has caught Him off-guard is comforting when we are facing what seems to be impossible.

Keep in mind, He is glorified by our promotions, in the same way you and I are honored by the kingdom successes of our children. "For your offspring will have influence and honor to prevail on your behalf!" (Psalm 127:5, TPT). I benefit spiritually in all of my children's successes. Something works to my favor whenever they become more Christlike. As we stand in our place of fulfilled destinies, we reveal Him as Father. A good, good Father.

**Rejection**

If I can't handle rejection with grace and kindness, I will not be able to enjoy the level of acceptance that God has in store for me. These challenges help to purify the soul so that blessings don't destroy us. In fact, all of God's disciplines are so His blessings don't kill us.

I know we all think we can handle blessing well, longing for it as we do. But without refined hearts through trial, blessing creates entitlement. It's only through humility and thankfulness that blessing empowers us unto righteousness, instead of driving us into self-centeredness.

Israel is a prime Old Testament example of this. Whenever they grew fat with blessing, they became careless in devotion. This is really the challenge of the hour we live in and the sole purpose of this book. To go where we need to go, to fully live out the significance we were born for, we must be able to carry the glory of God's favor without becoming self-absorbed. This we must learn to do to the glory of God.

It's vital to learn to navigate life with the knowledge that some have rejected us and it's OK. Rejection often reveals how much we depend on the approval of others for our self-esteem. It brings these things to the surface. Not so we carry shame, but so we see the weakness of our position and move to stable ground, which is based on how God thinks of us. Whenever insecurity is exposed, wrong security is exposed. It's an invitation to change.

Being able to handle rejection well doesn't mean I become calloused to the feelings of others. It means I recognize my need to hear and see from God's perspective. That must be the foundation of my identity.

**Criticism**

If I can't manage my heart with nobility and grace during times of criticism, I'll never be able to endure the praise He would like to send my way.

No one likes to be criticized, and often, what is said is downright cruel. Thanks to social media, I doubt there's ever been a time that criticism has been more prolific than it is now. And yet even here, we find that God is able to take something dishonoring and destructive and turn it into a moment of promotion. (There's a big difference between the criticism received from a friend and a total stranger in the media. As a way of protecting your heart, stay away from destructive comments.)

I once thanked a well-known person for opposing me in ministry by writing against me in a book. It wasn't that I felt he was right. In my opinion, he wasn't close. Nor did I think it would add insight or strength to the body of Christ. But it gave me an opportunity to grow, and I thanked him for it. The adverse winds he created gave me the opportunity to manage my heart and speech in a way that would take me closer to where God wants me to be. I've prayed the big prayers. They all require great character and stability in order to receive and manage the outcome well. His book gave me a wonderful chance to do just that.

---

If I don't live by the praises of men, I won't die by their criticisms. *#bornforsignificance*

---

Jesus was criticized, and He was perfect. How can I expect to go through life unscathed by criticism when I am so far from perfect? It's an unreasonable expectation, unless, of course, you do nothing with your life. Those who do nothing offend few.

Some might question my claim that God wants us praised. Because our use of the word *praise* is usually something done in a worship service, it's a harder concept to grasp. We know that God certainly is not setting us up to be worshiped. And yet He is the One who will say, "Well done, good and faithful servant." That's praise. Another term we could use here is the word *honor.* God desires us to be honored when we've become honorable. Honor given to the honorable is divine justice. It is the recognition of the working of His grace in a person and responding accordingly.

And yet it's the fear of man that causes people to seek the praises of men. If I don't live by the praises of men, I won't die by their criticisms. The fear of man is one of the strongest ways to undermine a life of faith. It defiles the heart, which is the seat of faith. "How can you believe, when you receive glory from one another and you do not seek the glory that is from the *one and* only God?" (John 5:44). Great faith can endure great criticism because it is free from the fear of man.

**Betrayal**

Betrayal is probably the hardest of the five challenges I've listed that will make or break us. If I do not handle betrayal well, I cannot be trusted with the depth of loyal friendships God has designed for me. We are designed for community. We were made to belong.

---

While I don't believe God causes betrayal, He is big enough to use it. *#bornforsignificance*

---

We need to look no further than the life of Jesus with the ultimate betrayer, Judas Iscariot, to learn how this process works. I remind you, Jesus put Judas in charge of the treasury, knowing he had a weakness. Was it to shame him or give him a chance to address the weakness of his own heart? Of course, I believe the latter. Jesus washed all the disciples' feet, including Judas's. Even those with the possibility of betrayal in their hearts must be given an opportunity for change. Here is the account of that night.

> *The Lord Jesus in the night in which He was betrayed* took bread; and when He had given thanks, He broke it and said, "This is My body, which is for you; do this in remembrance of Me." In the same way He took the cup also after supper, saying, "This cup is the new covenant in My blood; do this, as often as you drink it, in remembrance of Me." For as often as you eat this bread and drink the cup, you proclaim the Lord's death until He comes.
>
> —1 Corinthians 11:23–26

This is one of the most stunning statements in all of Scripture. "On the night in which He was betrayed," He thought and acted for the sake of others when it would have been easy to serve Himself. He used the betrayal, even as it was happening in the betrayer's heart, to advance His disciples into their destinies and purpose. This band of brothers was being formed into the ultimate bond through this dark night of the soul, scarred by the betrayal of a trusted friend.

Notice that none of the other disciples realized Judas was the betrayer, even as it was happening. They all asked Jesus, "Am I the one?" Betrayal is almost always unexpected. That's what makes it so painful. And yet, while I don't believe God causes betrayal, He is big enough to use it. And if Jesus was able to benefit from such an injustice, so can I.

It's imperative that we learn to embrace the good, the bad, and the ugly parts of our journey, with trust in our hearts for the only One who is able to work these ingredients into the masterpiece He has in His heart for us.

## THE INVITATION

Each of these challenges is an invitation to promotion. We can RSVP by embracing a lifestyle of trust, refusing to be embittered toward those who cause this onslaught in our lives.

Managing our hearts well is the challenge of the day. Most promises from God are connected to our success in stewarding our inner world correctly.

One of the most-often quoted Scriptures is Ephesians 3:20. Look at it here: "Now to Him who is able to do far more abundantly beyond all that we ask or think, according to the power that works within us." Consider these descriptive words—*far more abundantly beyond all that we ask or think.* Paul uses this extreme description for good reason. Beyond all we ask is the reach of our prayer lives on our best day. And beyond all we think is the reach of our imagination, also on our best day. That's where God dwells: beyond!

And those two promises are ours, with one condition. It is according to His power working in us. To the degree I allow Him to work deep in me, He will work beyond the reach of my prayers and imagination.

---

Managing our hearts well is the challenge of the day. Most promises from God are connected to our success in stewarding our inner world correctly. *#bornforsignificance*

---

Once again, we come face to face with this reality. Our inner world has an effect on the transformation of our outer world. We all want to see the transformation of our cities and nations. But in reality, it comes down to this: A transformed mind transforms a person. A transformed person transforms a city. And a transformed city transforms a nation. The seed that grows into the transformation of the world first begins in the heart of the believer who says yes to the purposes of God, no matter what.

We must determine to use our negative experiences well so that they can become the seeds to our resurrected futures.

I would never say those who have made wrong choices regarding these challenges for their lives aren't valuable or aren't good people. It's just that the kinds of dreams we all have and prayers we all pray require deep character. Character is the container for blessing. A weak container loses what it was given. "An inheritance gained hurriedly at the beginning will not be blessed in the end" (Prov. 20:21).

Too much too soon is certain defeat. Rarely are our character and maturity where they need to be to survive the blessings that we've asked of God. That's why we need discipline and the chance to learn enduring prayer. Persistent prayer is not to change God's mind about a matter. In fact, we are the ones who are changed in the posture of persistent prayer. Enduring prayer precedes our most significant promotions in life.

Sometimes our breakthroughs are proportioned to us according to what we have become in our inner world. Some may automatically think I mean this always takes years. Not necessarily. Radical, passionate prayers of persistence change us. And what might normally take years in shaping our inner world takes a brief season once we've entered the place of deep encounter with God.

Our inner world is shaped by our values, desires, thoughts, and intentions. How we manage ourselves during the most challenging situations often determines the measure of breakthrough and fulfillment we can handle in life without thinking of ourselves in an unhealthy, un-Christlike way. In mercy He withholds the answers that would crush us, choosing instead to lead us into significance through the way of the cross. I remind you, the resurrection always follows the cross. Significance can only be discovered His way, following His lead.

## CHAPTER 9

# GROOMING THROUGH DIFFICULTY

The subject of promotion is common in the average workplace. We go from one position of responsibility to another. Greater authority and income usually accompany these promotions. The corporate ladder is somewhat logical in the way it works. And while I don't want to say promotions in the kingdom are illogical, it sometimes appears that way.

In this chapter, we'll look at the unusual ways God promoted His own, turning average people into world changers. And while not everyone in our day receives a title, we do all need to belong, and we need to know our lives have significance.

One such passage where this is evident is 2 Samuel 7:8, "Thus says the Lord of hosts, 'I took you from the pasture, from following the sheep, to be ruler over My people Israel.'" *Remember our discussion in chapter 1 about dichotomies in the kingdom of God? We find these seemingly contradictory qualities again in this story.* When God was looking for a good leader, He wanted someone who was a good follower. David followed his sheep, and that qualified him for this task. Of course, there is more to the story and much more in the making of this great leader. But this one thing was worthy of God's emphasis in Scripture.

Finding someone who is moved by the needs of others means leadership will not be simply by the book. It will be by the heart. Leading from the heart is the challenge of the day. David's ability to be moved to provide, serve, and attend to the needs of sheep is, in part, what qualified him to be king of Israel.

It ought to be stated at this point that promotion is not about being elevated into positions of self-absorption. Such increase is always an increase in responsibility. From this point on, I will use words like *promotion*, *blessing*, *favor*, *increase*, and *leadership* interchangeably, as they emphasize different aspects of significance.

## CUT THE DRAMA

The extent of a person's influence and leadership can often be measured by what it takes to offend them. While I don't like it when people use this excuse to be rude and abrasive, the point remains, and it remains true. True leaders, those who have embraced their promotion well, are not easily offended. But those who live a life of entitlement through their promotion often express drama when things don't go their way.

You've heard the word *drama queen*. Often when people become rich and famous, they become overly dramatic about the slightest wrongs in life. People become connoisseurs of personal pleasure and can easily taste when someone has altered their recipe for an entitled lifestyle. They become outraged over an improperly cooked steak or the slightest shade difference in a room being painted. I love excellence and strive for this in every possible place in my life. But excellence never requires us to sacrifice the dignity of another person to obtain what we want.

## JESUS INSULTS

Many stories are hard to explain. We love to put Jesus in a predictable role where we have some measure of ownership and understanding. But Jesus seems to destroy those concepts quite quickly with even a casual glance at the Gospels. Let's look at one such story.

---

Excellence never requires us to sacrifice the dignity of another person to obtain what we want. *#bornforsignificance*

---

A woman who was not a Jew came to Jesus for a miracle. Her daughter was tormented and sick and was in much need of deliverance. When the mother came to Jesus, He didn't want to pray for her little girl.

> But after hearing of Him, a woman whose little daughter had an unclean spirit immediately came and fell at His feet. Now the woman was a Gentile, of the Syrophoenician race. And she kept asking Him to cast the demon out of her daughter. And He was saying to her, "Let the children be satisfied first, for it is not good to take the children's bread and throw it to the dogs." But she answered and said to Him, "Yes, Lord, but even the dogs under the table feed on the children's crumbs." And He said to her, "Because of this answer go; the demon has gone out of your daughter." And going back to her home, she found the child lying on the bed, the demon having left.
>
> —Mark 7:25–30

First of all, it says, "She kept asking," implying He ignored her for quite a while. Then He answered in a way that would seem inappropriate by our standards. If this story were to happen today, there would be outrage over His seemingly racist remarks. In appearance, He preferred His race over hers. Then He called her people *dogs*. It really doesn't help much that the word *dogs* can be translated *puppies*. Churches have split over less.

---

The kingdom of God is often on the other side of offense. *#bornforsignificance*

---

Of course, we now understand that Jesus had to fulfill His commission by ministering to the Jews first, but this is after the fact. How was this experience while it was happening? And was name-calling a necessary part of the journey? I think so.

God prepares us for increase by seeing what measure of rejection we can handle. The strength to carry promotion well is proven by how we respond to rejection and accusation. If my strength is questionable in this phase, my increase will be measured accordingly.

The Syrophoenician woman needed a hurdle to go over that she might break into the reality of the kingdom for her daughter's miracle. The kingdom of God is often on the other side of offense. Leaping over this hurdle brought her into the realm of miracles. She successfully passed this test, showing her resolve to be unoffended for the sake of her daughter. And that was a kingdom perspective coming from one who seemingly didn't qualify, as she was a non-Jew. Her answer came from her perception of Jesus' nature and process. This positioned her for a breakthrough.

## THE DANGER OF FATIGUE

Elijah was tired and a bit discouraged. He just had the most significant breakthrough of his entire prophetic ministry. It was a spectacular event, where fire came down from heaven, consuming his sacrifice, proving to the whole nation that God was truly God and Elijah was His prophet. This culminated with the killing of 850 demonized devil worshippers who had contaminated an entire nation with their false gods. (See 1 Kings 18.)

This triumphant day was followed by news that Jezebel had made a vow to kill Elijah. (See 1 Kings 19:2.) He despaired of life through a rumor. It's hard to imagine the courage it took to be victorious in the Mount Carmel experience with the false prophets. No doubt, fatigue had an effect on his perception of what happened next.

We know that pressure, trials, and conflicts can drain us emotionally. But it is also true that emotional highs put a demand on our inner world that is not always recognized. Many great ministers have made their worst mistakes following their most significant breakthroughs in ministry. Perhaps it's because we are tempted to become careless when the blessing of God is on us so abundantly. Elijah was in that very position. He now wanted to die.

Regardless, Elijah ran away into the wilderness where he had an encounter with an angel. The angel cooked a couple of meals for him, enabling him to travel a great distance to a cave. The Lord spoke to Him uniquely through a still, small voice. But he was still very discouraged. As a result of this interaction, God told him who to anoint to take his place. This meant Elijah would have someone to work with and for him for a season. This partnership would enable him to recover the strength he had lost in the last season. It is vital for us to see and understand how God-given connections strengthen our lives.

## ELIJAH CHOOSES AND REJECTS ELISHA

Elijah does as the Lord instructs him to do with this young man. But he adds a unique twist, as recorded in 1 Kings 19:19–20.

> So he departed from there and found Elisha the son of Shaphat, while he was plowing with twelve pairs of oxen before him, and he with the twelfth. And Elijah passed over to him and threw his mantle on him. He left the oxen and ran after Elijah and said, "Please let me kiss my father and my mother, then I will follow you." And he said to him, "Go back again, for what have I done to you?"

Elijah performed the most coveted act for this young man, Elisha. He threw his mantle upon him, which represented his call and ministry. When Elisha responded with his big yes, Elijah responded with, "Go back again, for what have I done to you?"

Elijah chose him by throwing his mantle over his shoulders. But then he played down his action as meaningless. For Elisha to carry this mantle, he had to be more concerned with God's choosing him than with Elijah's. The fear of man—even a great man or woman—can be a snare to those representing the King and His kingdom.

The young man ignored the prophet's response, knowing what had just taken place was from God, and no one could keep him from his call and destiny. He responded by burning the bridge to his past; he slaughtered his yoke of oxen (his employment) and gave the meat to the people. Then he arose and followed the man of God and served him well.

Elisha passed the first test. Now Elijah was confident he could handle the pressure of his position, at least in measure. But there was more.

## DISTRACTED BY PROMOTION

Elisha served well and became known as the one who washed Elijah's hands. There were many young prophets in that day, and it appears that they all would have done anything to be in Elisha's position. Being a servant under Elijah was better than being a master somewhere else. And Elisha knew it. But the big test was coming next.

As we fast forward to the day Elijah was going to die, all the prophets knew it. Prophetic communities are that way. It's tough to keep a secret. We have found that to be true in our own community, which is both frustrating and humorous.

---

Sometimes we settle for the inferior in our efforts to feel significant. It's not bad; it's just not best. *#bornforsignificance*

---

The next test was the greatest because it was a test of promotion. If Elisha had settled for any of the opportunities that Elijah was giving him, he never would have entered his potential. First, Elijah took him to Gilgal. Had he stayed there, he would have had a great ministry as Elijah's successor. The same happened when they went to Bethel and then Jericho. Each of these places represented promotion in position and status. But Elisha's heart ached for something different. So they finally passed through the Jordan River to his place of destiny.

Please note, it was only after Elisha turned down these opportunities to establish his own reputable ministry in these locations that Elijah asked him what he wanted. Sometimes we settle for the inferior in our efforts to feel significant. It's not bad; it's just not *best*. In the story of Elisha, we are reminded to follow our God-given passions beyond what anyone thinks is reasonable.

## GO BIG OR GO HOME

Elisha has already proven his humble heart by serving the prophet. He has also revealed his resistance to the fear of man in his initial calling. So when Elijah poses this final question, we see what has been growing in his heart all these years. Double! "I want a double portion of your spirit!" (See 2 Kings 2:9.) Elijah was quick to point out that this request was a tough one. He would now face the most unusual test. Elisha had to see Elijah when he was taken up. Then he would receive what he asked for. If not, he didn't qualify for the promotion.

---

In the story of Elisha, we are reminded to follow our God-given passions beyond what anyone thinks is reasonable. *#bornforsignificance*

---

I have found that if you know you're in a test, it's a much easier test than when you don't. All those tests are "open book" tests. For example, when the king was instructed to strike the ground with arrows, he didn't know his passion was being tested. He just thought it was an obedience issue.

> Then he said, "Take the arrows," and he took them. And he said to the king of Israel, "Strike the ground," and he struck it three times and stopped. So the man of God was angry with him and said, "You should have struck five or six times, then you would have struck Aram until you would have destroyed it. But now you shall strike Aram only three times."
>
> —2 Kings 13:18–19

When the king struck the ground only three times, the prophet got angry. He went on to explain that they would now have only three temporary victories because of his lack of zeal. But if he had struck the ground five or six times, they would have annihilated their enemy. Once the king realized he was being tested, it would have been easy for him to ask to take the test over and strike the ground a hundred times if needed. But the test was over. The passion of his heart had been revealed.

Now it was Elisha's turn. His one assignment seems simple enough, except for one thing. God was giving the test. And He always looks for answers that reveal the heart. He looks for purity, passion, and focus. Let the games begin.

> As they were going along and talking, behold, there appeared a chariot of fire and horses of fire which separated the two of them. And Elijah went up by a whirlwind to heaven. Elisha saw it and cried out, "My father, my father, the chariots of Israel and its horsemen!" And he saw Elijah no more. Then he took hold of his own clothes and tore them in two pieces. He also took up the mantle of Elijah that fell from him and returned and stood by the bank of the Jordan. He took the mantle of Elijah that fell from him and struck the waters and said, "Where is the Lord, the God of Elijah?" And when he also had struck the waters, they were divided here and there; and Elisha crossed over.
>
> —2 Kings 2:11–14

Perhaps you've heard a sermon on or the old hymn about Elijah being taken to heaven in a chariot of fire. It didn't happen. He was taken up in a whirlwind. What were the chariot of fire and horses all about? They were God-sent, supernatural distractions to see if Elisha would stay the course with his assignment, which was to see Elijah when he was taken up.

If he could not pass the test, he would still be Elijah's heir apparent. He would be the most respected prophet of the day. But the double portion would not be his. The level of anointing he was asking for would cause problems if he could be distracted by God-given activities outside of his assignment. It's one thing to survive distractions of the flesh and sin. It's quite another to survive one as glorious as heaven invading earth in this way. But because it was not his assignment, he had to fight to keep his focus. He did. And the rest is history.

Elisha picked up the mantle that fell from heaven, and he struck the waters like Elijah had done, asking, "Where is the God of Elijah?" The waters parted. Elisha discovered where the God of Elijah was. He was now with him. Elisha had just received the most significant promotion of any prophet in history, and he performed exactly twice as many miracles as his father Elijah—the prototype of the ultimate prophet, John the Baptist.

Two unusual hurdles—rejection and promotion—were given to Elisha that he might enter this wonderful place of perfect significance. The passion for the double portion did not come from a prophetic word given to him when the mantle was placed on his shoulders. That desire was released to him because it was first burning on the inside. Of course, it was God who put it there. But he faithfully carried that fire unto fulfillment, which is rare and costly. Elisha succeeded where few others do.

## CHAPTER 10

# THE BACK DOOR TO THE THRONE ROOM

PROMOTION CONNECTS US to our purpose and almost always leads us to greater influence. And while you may or may not desire a leadership role, in essence, that is what's at stake. Not all positions of leadership come with a title. But leadership does mean you have influence, your decisions affect others, and people follow your example and instructions.

David is a wonderful case study for this process. His life provides us with a brilliant roadmap to promotion in a biblical sense, and his failures give insight to the perils that come with increased responsibilities.

Not all positions of leadership come with a title. But leadership does mean you have influence, your decisions affect others, and people follow your example and instructions. *#bornforsignificance*

## DAVID WASN'T COUNTED

David wasn't included in his father's line up of sons to be blessed by the prophet Samuel. It reminds me somewhat of the little boy whose lunch was used to feed the multitude in John 6. It says there were five thousand men. They didn't count the women or the children in that day. It was a cultural value of men only. It is strange but true. While the people of the day didn't count the little boy, Jesus did. And the lunch from the one who didn't count became the seed for the miracle. God sees all, and no system can keep Him from promoting the one He wants to promote.

David found himself in a similar position. His father Jesse was asked to bring his sons before the prophet Samuel, so he lined them all up—except David. Samuel looked at each one, waiting for the approval of God for this next promotion. They all looked like possible king material by outward appearance. But God reminded Samuel that He looks on the heart. So Samuel asked Jesse if he had any more sons, to which Jesse replied he did, but his youngest son, David, was taking care of the sheep. At Samuel's request, he brought David before him. God spoke to the prophet, "This is the one!" The one who was overlooked by his family became the one sought for by God. Samuel recognized the hand of God upon him and anointed him king of Israel.

---

Delayed answers groom us to be capable of receiving God's response without it destroying us. *#bornforsignificance*

---

The Spirit of God was removed from Saul. He disqualified himself by his rebellion against God (1 Sam. 16:14.) Conversely, the Spirit of God came upon David (v. 13), whom God trusted to be king over Israel. He recognized David was a man after His heart.

It appears that David used his time of caring for his father's sheep as a time to be with God. Much of his learning about the ways of God was formed in those hours in the wilderness giving praise to God on his harp. It was probably in this environment where David learned the important concepts that would later shape his values and decisions as king—most notably, that God inhabited his praise and that God valued the contrite heart over the sacrifice of animals. This worshipping shepherd was given insights into the heart of God that helped make him the greatest king in Israel's history. David was moved by what he learned of God's ways, and he patterned his heart and values after God's own heart. This is his greatest legacy.

Even though David was anointed king by the prophet Samuel, it would be many years before he ascended to the throne. Delayed answers groom us to be capable of receiving God's response without it destroying us. The discipline of the Lord enables us to step into the fulfillment of God's Word over our lives without failing because of *gaining an inheritance too quickly*. (See Proverbs 20:21.)

## COURAGE CAUSES TROUBLE

As a young man, David had killed a lion and a bear to protect the sheep. No wonder God wanted him to lead the people He loved. David willingly put himself in danger to protect his assignment, which perfectly qualified him for promotion. What he did when no one was watching qualified him to beat Goliath when two nations were watching. It's not that we seek to be noticed; it's that God would find us trustworthy to be noticed. Recognition adds pressure that not everyone can handle well. David passed with flying colors.

Goliath was taunting the armies of God. Saul was paralyzed

with fear, as were the rest of the armies of Israel. David was delivering food to his brothers in the army when he heard the commotion caused by this evil giant. His brothers became angry with him when he asked about the problem. Their lack of courage became evident when David spoke without fear concerning that Philistine. I'm sure they attributed David's courage to his youth. But in fact, he had been groomed for this moment, and his God-shaped courage rose to the occasion.

It's interesting to note that the people who lacked the courage to fight Goliath were the same ones who criticized the one who had what they didn't have. Jealousy surfaces in the most awkward situations. Sometimes we react to situations having to do with other people, thinking we are functioning in great zeal and discernment, when in fact, jealousy has gripped our souls. Staying tender before the Lord safeguards all of us in this regard.

David persuaded King Saul to let him fight Goliath. David picked up five stones because Goliath had brothers. His faith extended through his present challenge into his future. But once Goliath was killed, all the Philistines fled. The taunting, potential problems of our future often run when we face our moment with great courage. It appears that David's harshest critics became his supporters after his victory and gladly served with him in the army of King Saul.

## JEALOUSY'S SPEAR POINT

David was brought into the king's house, where he became best friends with Saul's son Jonathan. Kings like to be around winners, and David qualified. But winners bring stuff to the surface in those who are insecure. Saul's fear of what the people thought became a snare in his own heart, revealing deep issues that were to become his downfall.

Over time David's courage became the talk of the town, invading the lyrics of the music of their day. The women were heard singing, "Saul has slain his thousands, and David his tens of thousands" (1 Sam. 18:7). Jealousy filled Saul's heart, and he sought to kill David. Jealousy is a devastating emotional ailment fed by faulty reasoning. It causes one to covet the honor or recognition another is receiving, discounting that person's worthiness.

---

Kings like to be around winners. But winners bring stuff to the surface in those who are insecure. *#bornforsignificance*

---

Saul tried to kill David with a spear. He missed, but he continued his efforts, rejecting the pleas of his son to reconsider. He hunted David like an animal for well over ten years. The rejection David suffered at this point came from the king himself, although Jonathan remained his loyal friend.

Saul and his army chased David. There were many hair-raising moments as David spent years running from this once important father figure turned murderous madman. Let's face it, when someone is determined to kill you, it shapes your character. When that someone is also a king with resources and spies who could be rewarded for information, it either shapes your character or drives you a little crazy. This very undesirable situation became the "school of kings" for David.

We should never be surprised by what God is able and willing to use to train us for our purpose in life. This future king now had the responsibility to hold on to God's word in the midst of prevailing circumstances that contradicted what was spoken over his life. The choice for all of us is simple: either we allow the word over our lives to be affected by our circumstances, or we affect the circumstances with the word. David knew he was made with a destiny and held fast.

Most of us have dreams and words spoken over our lives that seem impossible. They have to be, or we would think we could accomplish them on our own. I'm sure that being anointed king by someone as respectable as the prophet Samuel helped David in his challenging season. But let's face it, being hunted by a madman had to seem like he was going in the opposite direction to the word of the prophet over his life.

## REJECTION THAT MATTERS

All rejection hurts. But some rejections hurt deeper than others. In David's case, he became a fugitive because of Saul's madness. While on the run, he found a place to stay for a season, in a village called Keilah. This was a community that David had saved from the Philistines. They no doubt had value for this military leader because of their own well-being.

---

Most of us have dreams and words spoken over our lives that seem impossible. They have to be, or we would think we could accomplish them on our own. *#bornforsignificance*

---

When David found out that Saul knew he was in hiding there, he asked God if his own Jewish brothers would betray him and turn him over to Saul. God told him they would turn him over and that Saul was coming to kill him. It has to hurt even more when the people who owe you their lives turn on you in your moment of need. But people bound by fear usually reject their chance at nobility. David left the protection of the community for the wilderness.

## FROM REJECTION TO A CHURCH OF REJECTS

People began to gather around David during his time of exile. First Samuel 22:2 says, "Everyone who was in distress, and everyone who was in debt, and everyone who was discontented" began to follow David. For some reason, I see the *Star Wars* bar scene whenever I read this verse. These are guys who don't fit in anywhere. Their personal issues make this group the least desirable church to pastor. And yet this was the start of an extraordinary miracle.

David demonstrated the heart of royalty before he had the title by embracing these men with their issues. He trained them for life and warfare to become what God intended. David's father, Jesse, had obvious issues that were seen in his lack of desire to bring David before the prophet Samuel to see which son might be king. And when his potentially inspirational father in royalty, Saul, crumbled under pressure, David himself remained strong.

Under his leadership, these misfits became known as the mighty men of David and were spoken of with honor in 2 Samuel 23. Their military conquests are without equal. And while I hate war of every kind, I would love to see the video of the battles these men won. They're absolutely stunning. At least four of these men also killed giants. As disciples of David, they give evidence to this principle: *If you want to kill giants, follow a giant-killer.*

## LIVING IN THE ENEMY'S CAMP

Eventually, no doubt for safety's sake, David moved his group to the land of the Philistines, where their king gave him the city of Ziklag. The mighty men of David were at least thirty-seven in number but could have been closer to fifty, depending on how we interpret the descriptions given in Scripture. They also had families, so this move no doubt provided them with a chance at creating stability for their households too.

The Philistines took a liking to David, who would raid the enemies of Israel at night. These were also the enemies of the Philistines, so they thought David's conquests were actually for them and that he was a strength to their own military cause. But when the Philistines decided to go to war with Israel, some of their leaders refused to allow David to fight with them. Their reasoning was that David could turn on them in the midst of the battle and Israel would want him as their king.

In this moment of rejection, David turned to go back home. Off in the distance, they saw the worst situation imaginable: Ziklag was burning with fire. When they came hastily into the city, what they feared the most had happened. All their wives and children were gone, along with all their possessions. The circumstances of these men who struggled with the daily issues of life had just started to get ahead, so to speak, and now it appeared to be over. Pain gave way to fear, and fear was happy to take over.

---

The choice for all of us is simple: Either we allow the word over our lives to be affected by our circumstances, or we affect the circumstances with the word. *#bornforsignificance*

---

These mighty men wept until they had no more strength. These hardened soldiers, known for their military conquests, had developed compassionate hearts, at least for their own families. This was no doubt a result of David's leadership in their lives. If David was anything, he was a man of the heart.

In exhaustion and fear, the men talked among themselves about killing David. It's a shocking part of the story but really shouldn't take us by surprise. The same thing is done today. When people are in pain or frustration, it's common to blame the one in charge. Professional sports teams fire managers. Nations vote for the other party. The point is, we rarely make an effort to take personal responsibility for the loss. It's easier to blame the guy at the top.

Here is the worst moment imaginable, yet it reveals that David is now ready to be king. The Bible says, "But David strengthened himself in the LORD his God" (1 Sam. 30:6).

## GROOMED BY REJECTION

Consider for a moment what David's life looked like at crucial moments in his life.

1. David was overlooked by his father and brothers. He was family, but he wasn't counted.
2. David was rejected by King Saul, who jealously tried to kill him. David helped establish the kingdom for Saul by his military victories, but it didn't count.
3. David was rejected by his brethren at Keilah when they purposed to turn him over to Saul. David delivered them from the Philistines, but they forgot.

4. He was rejected by the Philistines when he wasn't allowed to go to war with them. David was a benefit to their nation, but it didn't matter under pressure.
5. He was rejected by his own men when they spoke of killing him. David had turned their lives around. They owed him their lives, their success, and their hope for tomorrow. They lost sight of his value to them in their pain.

David was experiencing a moment that most of us would claim to be the darkest moment of our lives. His lowest point became the moment he proved what he was made of. Instead of becoming angry at the mighty men, instead of pointing out the error of their ways, he came to them with a plan. He didn't punish them. He didn't avoid their pain. He simply acted like the king he was in his heart and led them into a great victory.

The Bible says they recovered all. All their family members. All their possessions. All. Restored completely. (See 1 Samuel 30:8.)

## THE BACK DOOR

It's not an accident that in the next part of the story, David became king. At his lowest point, he strengthened himself. I personally believe that at times God will deafen our closest friends to our heart's cry that we might be forced to learn this vital lesson: how to bring strength to ourselves. He would never do this to build independence and isolation into our lives. But leaders—those who have longed for God's promotion—must learn how to minister to themselves. It was from this place of *aloneness* that David passed the final test on his readiness to rule.

---

I personally believe that at times God will deafen our closest friends to our heart's cry that we might be forced to learn how to bring strength to ourselves. *#bornforsignificance*

---

While the Bible doesn't give us a list of what David did to strengthen himself, it does give us glimpses into his values, lifestyle, and thoughts. The psalms do this beautifully. When I had to learn this skill of strengthening myself, for my own sanity, I learned much from his example. (I've written an entire book on this subject: *Strengthen Yourself in the Lord* by Destiny Image.) These are the things I do continually:

1. *Worship.* There's nothing like the manifest presence of God upon a person to recalibrate what is important and what is not. There is unlimited life and strength in His presence. I put special emphasis on giving thanks and praise in the very areas I have need. These are given as a sacrifice and not merely tokens of my convenience. In other words, I exalt and honor Him for being my faithful provider whenever I'm in need of provision. I thank Him for the answer before it comes. Such actions help to bring about a change in perspective, which is essential in being strong enough to face my problems well.
2. *Promises.* I review the prophetic words over my life, as well as the portions of Scripture God has

used at significant moments in my life to give me hope and a promise. I spend considerable time reviewing these words. I can't afford to have a thought in my head about me that God doesn't have in His. This form of biblical meditation is vital to ensure I live in His strength. Joshua 1:5–9 illustrates this part of the journey quite well.

3. *Friends.* I purposely choose to spend time with faith-filled friends. It's not so we can talk about problems. I just find their humor and view of life to be refreshing for me. At the same time, I restrict my time with people who drain me. There are times when those kinds of people are not a problem because I'm living from the abundance of grace on my life. But during times of distress, when rejection seems to be at every turn, I restrict whom I spend time with. There's no sense in deliberately choosing to be with people who make my fight of faith even more difficult.

The Bible is filled with examples of people who faced great impossibilities and overcame the odds through simple faith and obedience. Both faith and obedience are measured through actions. Alone, they are just theories, but when we act, they are confirmed and solidified. For me, it's like two-part epoxy. It only works when both elements are combined.

## THE GIFT OF REJECTION

It sounds strange, I'm sure, but these kinds of challenges in life can be considered a gift. While I don't believe God orchestrates catastrophes for our lives, He does stand with us, giving us hope and promises that are always greater than the problem.

To those untrained in the ways of the King and His kingdom, it could appear that these moments are setbacks, when in fact they are shortcuts to promotion if navigated well. They are the crash courses in the school of the kingdom, ensuring that we are capable of surviving and thriving in our area of promotion. Because of this, we can, with sincerity of heart, be thankful for these moments of rejection. They became the potter's hands that shaped David, the man with a right heart, into the greatest king in Israel's history. What all of us would have rejected and renounced became the back door for promotion.

---

While I don't believe God orchestrates catastrophes for our lives, He does stand with us, giving us hope and promises that are always greater than the problem. *#bornforsignificance*

---

I learned through a personal trial several years ago that God is looking for our trust. I wanted to express bold faith. Through this season, I came to a conclusion that had previously escaped me: *Bold faith stands on the shoulders of quiet trust.* His faithfulness is so perfect and complete that I owe Him nothing less than absolute trust, regardless of my circumstances. This approach becomes the back door to promotion.

The process that God uses to take us into our destiny is entirely for our sakes. There is no punishment involved. Without the training and tests, we would certainly fall in the most destructive way—destructive to ourselves and those around us. It is certainly God's mercy that withholds until the time is right. The perils of promotion, the essential ingredient of our significance, are not so frightening if the process was fully embraced. Examining the perils will help us to see the warning signs, be fully restored in the proper kind of "fear of God," and give ourselves completely for the glory of God, His way.

# PART III

# THE PERILS OF PROMOTION

## CHAPTER 11

# THE CHALLENGE OF BLESSING

IT IS NEARLY impossible to find anytime in history when a great move of God increased in momentum and significance as it passed from one generation to the next. In fact, I don't know of this ever happening in church history. And yet it should have countless times.

People often assume that because a time of blessing or revival ended, it was God's will for it to end. They assume that is the heart of God because of how people have responded to God and not the nature of God's promise for our lives. But God is never defined by people's response to Him. Otherwise, the healing of the ten lepers would have been a failure, since only one returned to give thanks. Only one had the true transformation of heart to respond appropriately to God. God is revealed in His work, not our response to His work.

Continual increase is in God's nature, taking us from glory to glory, from faith to faith. In Jesus' teaching on stewardship, with the minas and the talents, increase was required. God expects us to increase and grow in whatever He gives us. When one generation receives a spiritual inheritance from the previous generation, they are given an opportunity to go where the previous generation didn't have the time to go. And yet, even though this is always the possibility, it has never been the norm.

Great moves of God require a life of great risk, along with the willingness to be scorned and rejected by peers. Perhaps it's that the children of spiritual champions try to approach significance and impact another way. They often build monuments in the memory of their spiritual fathers and mothers as their expression of honor, but seldom take the move of God to another level.

---

God is never defined by people's response to Him. #bornforsignificance

---

While this book is not about revival, it is about the promotion and increase that God brings about in all of our lives. And the subject of the great moves of God illustrates the challenge of blessings.

## THE EXCEPTION

The transition from David's rule to that of his son Solomon provides the only time in history that I am aware of when God-given significance and greatness is followed by a generation that takes it further than the previous. It's a brilliant example of culture and society going from glory to glory. I'm not saying it's never happened, either in the Bible or church history. I'm just saying it's not common, and frankly, I've never seen it.

Solomon's failures were all the more devastating because of this. The greater the significance of a person, the greater the effect of their failures on those under their influence. But suffice it to say, promotion must be handled with care.

## CONTRADICTION IN ROLES

Solomon was the most powerful king ever. But the momentum for his greatness came from his father, King David. It was David who set the stage for his son's promotion. It's important to realize we seldom enter true significance on our own. Someone will be used by God to lay the foundation for us to build on.

King David was a blessed man. As I mentioned earlier, he was all heart—known for his passions and not just his disciplines. This was evident in His love for God. He was willing to look foolish to his subjects in order to express all that was in his heart for the One he loved with reckless abandon. His dancing before the Lord embarrassed his wife Michal. She feared what people might think. He didn't. David danced for the audience of One. Truly courageous people must put aside the fear of man and live in fear of God. This is the only way to fully enter purpose and ultimate promotion.

David's heart was also seen in his passion for enforcing justice by obtaining the rest of God's Promised Land for Israel. They had gone hundreds of years being seemingly satisfied with less than what God had promised. But David would have nothing to do with lack, leading his army in victory after victory that they might obtain all that God had promised. This was pure, unadulterated passion for God that could be measured in his love for His people and his desire for divine justice.

We can also recognize David's passion through his military accomplishments. They are legendary. You'll recall that he raised up men who were so mighty in battle that their achievements almost look like the work of angels and not men. Seriously. One man, Josheb-basshebeth, chief of the captains, fought against eight hundred soldiers, by himself, and killed them all. Another one, further down the Bible's list of greatness, Abishai, killed three hundred by himself. The point is, David was God's man for the hour. His military strength was God-given. God led him into battles to complete the assignment given to Joshua and previous generations that had never been fulfilled: fully obtaining the Promised Land. This illustrates the justice of God in an Old Testament context.

David longed to display his heart of passion for God and his desire to honor Him by building a place for Him to dwell, a house of God, a temple. But God wouldn't allow him to do so because he was a man of bloodshed. The Scripture doesn't say it was because of his sin with Bathsheba or his dealings with her husband, Uriah. God points to the general effect of his life of military prowess.

---

To have a lasting impact on humanity, we must be more than people who see problems. We must be people with solutions. *#bornforsignificance*

---

Most often, people think of God forbidding David to build the temple as a form of punishment for his murderous ways. I question that conclusion. It doesn't seem consistent with the fact that David fought wars that God led him into. God created him to be a military strength and to carry out the original command to drive out the enemies from their inheritance. So if it's not punishment, what is it? I believe the Lord is revealing the kind of ministry He builds with. God builds with *peace*, which is the meaning of Solomon's name.

Look at it this way: War removes the problem so the man of peace can build the solution. It's like clearing away a dilapidated building so builders can construct something new. Demolition crews are rarely, if ever, the construction crew needed to build again. Many ministries involve themselves with a war-type approach to ministry. They oppose their government as well as other churches when they violate what they think is correct. They confront their denominational leaders and anyone else who lacks the insights they carry. They are war- and conflict-minded.

This same group of leaders becomes frustrated with their inability to build something that is lasting. God doesn't tend to build on that foundation, as by nature, it is in conflict with what He is doing in the earth. David was necessary and important. But Solomon took his momentum to another level. Their assignments were different but complementary from a kingdom perspective.

To have a lasting impact on humanity, we must be more than people who see problems. We must be people with solutions. God is a creator; He's a builder. We get to share in His nature by co-laboring with His heart to answer every question and need carried by people around us.

## MAJOR TRANSITION

Whenever we enter into a promotion, it is a transition for everyone involved. For some reason, transitions rarely come without their own set of problems and challenges. It doesn't matter whether it's a promotion at work, an increase in anointing or spiritual gift, or a move to the other side of the country, transition is challenging. I can't think of any transition more extreme than that of David to Solomon, from the man of war to the man of peace.

Look at it this way. David was the man all nations feared. Solomon was the man the leaders of the nations wanted to be with. Israel transitioned from being feared to being admired, all because they had a king who received an unparalleled promotion in wisdom. The nations came to learn of his wisdom. Both David and Solomon were powerful, influential, and significant. But only one became the example and provided the insights that other nations could learn from.

All the men of the earth and all the kings of the known world came to sit at Solomon's feet to learn of his wisdom. What was the purpose? To better learn to rule their nations, bring prosperity to their people, and have longevity in their family lines. Practically speaking, Solomon taught them wisdom, which is divine reasoning. In a very real sense, they were exposed to the mind of Christ although they lived during the days of the old covenant. And they learned from this experience.

The prophets spoke of the nations coming to their light. It was God's intention long before Israel had any understanding of how it could work. I'm sure they thought if only they had great military power, nations would be drawn to them. But that didn't do it. That would have been fear-based hunger, not a genuine passion for learning. God knew that if He could put His wisdom in a person, the God-given appetite for wisdom would surface in the hearts of people, and they would do anything to get it. Perhaps an often-overlooked miracle is the fact that kings humbled themselves in their pursuit of wisdom by leaving their place of glory, prestige, and honor to sit at the feet of another king. Only God-given hunger will do that. Our promotion is intended to put us before people in such a way that they see the nature of God and long to know Him.

Sometime later the prophet Micah declared that people would come to the people of God for solutions for life. "Many nations will come and say, 'Come and let us go up to the mountain of the Lord and to the house of the God of Jacob, that

He may teach us about His ways and that we may walk in His paths'" (4:2). This verse reveals the heart of God to draw all nations to Himself. But He uses us to attract them. What's interesting is that in Solomon's case, it was His unusual promotion in wisdom that brought the nations to him. What God did through Solomon, attract nations to Him, He is now going to do through His house, the church of the living God.

---

Our promotion is intended to put us before people in such a way that they see the nature of God and long to know Him. *#bornforsignificance*

---

Promotion on us is inviting to others. When God promotes us, it reveals His heart for mankind, drawing others to Him through us. It's not the money, title, or power that attracts as much as it is people functioning in their God-given role, happy in their own skin. This is why there is much to be said about this issue of "how we handle the promotion of the Lord."

## DELIVERED FROM MEDIOCRACY

*Mediocre* means average, while *cracy* means rule or government. The people of God are not to settle for living under the influence of *average*. Mediocracy takes on the nature of governmental power in setting boundaries for living that are contrary to the kingdom of God. The nature of God, revealed in ongoing increase, is supposed to be seen in how we think, plan, believe, pray, pursue, and steward.

I mentioned this earlier, and I'll repeat it here: as the people of God, we are to live with a realization that there is always more. We are part of an eternal kingdom, the wonder of whose limitlessness will take an eternity to reveal. This is never to promote anxiousness or legitimize *being driven* as an expression of the kingdom. Being driven is a poor substitute for the life of focus we were designed to live. The Scripture says we will be led forth with peace. This means I don't want to go anywhere that peace doesn't take me. Just as great faith comes from surrender and not striving, so the great experiences of promotion come from yieldedness as a lifestyle. Even when we are called to fight, as is also taught in Scripture, we fight from the victory of Christ at the cross and resurrection, not for it.

If there's anything Solomon was *not*, it's mediocre. He excelled in ways unknown before. Wisdom elevated him above what mortal humans are usually capable of experiencing. The divine, the mind of Christ, became manifest in one person at a level above anything heard of or seen before. Such is the nature of this gift that should be the heart-cry of every person alive. Wisdom is not simply having a gift for bringing solutions to human need, nor is it to elevate a person above others in the sense of superiority. It is the favor of God to illustrate heaven's blueprint to replace earthly chaos.

---

Just as great faith comes from surrender and not striving, so the great experiences of promotion come from yieldedness as a lifestyle. *#bornforsignificance*

---

Wisdom is also prophetic in nature in that it sees beyond the natural limitations of a subject. Let me illustrate wisdom in this way. Let's say you're looking at a typical wall in a home. What you normally see is sheetrock covered with wood, paint, or wallpaper. Wisdom sees beyond the obvious into the internal structure of something—in this case, the two-by-fours to which the sheetrock is attached. In other words, wisdom sees into the nature of a problem, challenge, or opportunity. It brokers the creative influence of God's nature into the cavernous condition of human brokenness and God-given potential.

## SOLOMON'S BEGINNING

One of the most impressive parts of Solomon's story is how it all started. He was visited by God in his sleep. Imagine God coming to you while you're sound asleep, giving you a wish where you can have anything you want. I remember as a child wanting to get that chance to have anything I wanted. That desire, without question, can be selfish in that it is "my will be done." But it is also true that God puts things in people's hearts that long for expression, such as Solomon's moment with God.

Remarkably, God trusted Solomon's request for wisdom, even though he made it while he was sleeping. What is it of God that we carry so deeply that God can trust our reasoning while we're asleep? And why is it that Solomon was the only one offered such a choice? Perhaps it was because he was the only one trained from childhood to make such a choice. Proverbs 4:3–5 reveals how David prepared his son for significance.

> When I was a son to my father, tender and the only son in the sight of my mother, then he taught me and said to me, "Let your heart hold fast my words; keep my commandments and live; acquire wisdom! Acquire understanding! Do not forget nor turn away from the words of my mouth."

Once again, we see the role that others play in our advancements in life. They must be remembered and honored. David prepared his son for this moment. I wonder if God might have been drawn to Solomon to offer him a wish because He knew he was the only one trained to make the right decision. Perhaps. We're obviously not robots programmed to make the right decisions. God makes Himself vulnerable in that He invites us into a relational journey where our wills have an influence on the outcome of things. In this case, Solomon responded to opportunity with a brilliant choice.

> Now Solomon loved the Lord, walking in the statutes of his father David, except he sacrificed and burned incense on the high places. The king went to Gibeon to sacrifice there, for that was the great high place; Solomon offered a thousand burnt offerings on that altar. In Gibeon the Lord appeared to Solomon in a dream at night; and God said, "Ask what *you wish* me to give you."
>
> Then Solomon said, "You have shown great lovingkindness to Your servant David my father, according as he walked before You in truth and righteousness and uprightness of heart toward You; and You have reserved for him this great lovingkindness, that You have given him a son to sit on his throne, as it is this day. Now, O Lord my God, You have made Your servant king in place of my father David, yet I am but a little child; I do not know how to go out or come in. Your servant is in the midst of Your people which You have chosen, a great people who are too many to be numbered or counted. So give Your servant an understanding heart to judge Your people to discern between good and evil. For who is able to judge this great people of Yours?"
>
> It was pleasing in the sight of the Lord that Solomon had asked this thing. God said to him, "Because you have asked this thing and have not asked for yourself long life, nor have asked riches for yourself, nor have you asked for the life of your enemies, but have asked for yourself discernment to understand justice, behold, I have done according to your words. Behold, I have given you a wise and discerning heart, so that there has been no one like you before you, nor shall one like you arise after you. I have also given you what you have not asked, both riches

> and honor, so that there will not be any among the kings like you all your days. If you walk in My ways, keeping My statutes and commandments, as your father David walked, then I will prolong your days."
>
> Then Solomon awoke, and behold, it was a dream. And he came to Jerusalem and stood before the ark of the covenant of the Lord, and offered burnt offerings and made peace offerings, and made a feast for all his servants.
>
> —1 Kings 3:3–15

I love this story and have great respect for Solomon. I'm also saddened that he didn't take note of the things he should have seen early on in his journey. His cry for wisdom was stunning. But he was raised by a man of God's presence. David was a man who valued the presence of God above all. It's easy to say that we value His presence, and yet this reality must be measured in the price we've paid to obtain and protect it. Each of us has the measure of God's presence that we're willing to jealously guard.

David's story reveals his appetite for God, his willingness to look foolish in the pursuit of His presence. His life reveals how he valued Him enough to cause the lives of all the priests to rotate around the privilege of ministering to Him 24/7. This is referred to as the Tabernacle of David. Had Solomon picked up this one value from his father, he could have avoided massive heartache for himself and the nation he served.

## WARNING SIGNS CAME EARLY

Take note of this initial warning and insight: "Now Solomon loved the Lord...except he sacrificed and burned incense on the high places" (v. 3). God is the One who directs our attention to the exception. He sacrificed on high places. Solomon's weakness begins to surface at the start of his story. He had great value for how things appeared to others. Other nations worshipped on high places. And while Solomon started by worshipping God there, it was still not according to the commands of God.

---

It's easy to say that we value His presence, and yet this reality must be measured in the price we've paid to obtain and protect it. *#bornforsignficance*

---

This weakness of developing worship around self-will became the point at which he brought in the worship of false gods. In a sense, it is impossible to worship God our own way. In reality, it becomes worshipping our own way. Self-will is not welcome in worship.

Solomon's sacrifices at Gibeon are the example of a man trying to find God. Yet the core of the gospel message is that it was God who was reaching out to us. Yielding our will to His is welcome and celebrated. Real worship is measured in surrender. God doesn't fit into our plan; we fit into His. He has a will. He has a design. He has a mind. Our delight is discovering what our Designer has planned for us.

The Bible says Solomon sacrificed a thousand animals to God in that place. But he didn't dance before God like his father. There is no record of his personal expression to God. His worship was impressive to others in that it was expensive and elaborate. But it was unimpressive to God because it didn't include Solomon offering himself.

That really is the goal of all worship: to become the offering. "You shall love the Lord your God with all your heart, and with all your soul, and with all your strength, and with all your mind" (Luke10:27). Quoted by Jesus in Luke, this command was first taught throughout the Old Testament.

In other words, Solomon would have been aware of this standard for our devotion to God. And yet his worship seems more like token worship. When we give tokens of worship, we do enough to ease the conscience, but not enough to transform our lives. David's dance, Mary's alabaster vial, the widow's mite, all speak of an external offering that represented true internal affection and surrender to a God who is perfect in beauty, goodness, and holiness. Solomon missed out on what should have been more natural to him than almost anyone else in history because of who his father was: David.

It must also be noted that God wasn't there—at least, not in the sense Israel was accustomed to. The ark of the covenant was in Jerusalem, which is where the presence of the almighty God resided for Israel. It wasn't figurative. He was there. God wasn't on the high place called Gibeon. Solomon had shifted the focus of worship from Mount Zion, where God was, to Gibeon, which had the appearance of where God should be.

What is interesting is that after God came to Solomon in the dream, he awakened and quickly returned to Jerusalem to the ark of the covenant. He appeared before the actual presence of God to give offerings. This shows us that He knew. He instinctively knew that in his moment of promotion and significance, he had to return to the presence of God and not settle for a form of worship that violated what God commanded.

This simple act of returning to Jerusalem shows us what he had learned from his father, David, but didn't keep in practice. It was the secret to David's success. But for Solomon, this was to become the not-so-secret cause of his failure.

Momentums are given to us in God. They must be recognized

and valued. What David gave his life for became insignificant for Solomon. Perhaps it was because he knew he had a different assignment than his father, which was true. But wisdom helps us to determine what to keep and what to replace. In this case, the man of war handed the baton to the man of peace. And it was the man of peace who desperately needed the presence of God to be his *due north* so that deception could not enter.

---

It is impossible to worship God our own way. In reality, it becomes worshipping our own way. *#bornforsignificance*

---

This exception of the high places became the fly in the ointment. And because it was not dealt with early on, it became the beginning of Solomon's downfall. Dealing with issues while they're small is so much easier than when they become fully developed with deep roots in our personality and lifestyle. Thankfully it's not impossible, but the repentance must be equal to the sin.

## EXPONENTIAL DOWNFALL

Solomon made a mistake similar to Adam in the Garden of Eden so many years earlier. Satan told Adam he would be like God if he ate the forbidden fruit. He already was! He tried to obtain by his works what God had provided by grace. And now Solomon was in the same position. He tried to obtain favor and peace with surrounding nations by marrying the daughters of the surrounding kings. Yet he already had favor and peace. These were the very ones who came to sit at his feet and learn wisdom.

Remember, Solomon had a need for public appearance that

secured his place of value in people's eyes. This can never become a focus for a true leader. It did for Solomon, and it became his Achilles' heel. Compromise and disobedience never release the kind of favor and increased blessing that will last. In fact, Solomon's choice would become the downfall of his throne.

> Now King Solomon loved many foreign women along with the daughter of Pharaoh: Moabite, Ammonite, Edomite, Sidonian, and Hittite women, from the nations concerning which the LORD had said to the sons of Israel, "You shall not associate with them, nor shall they associate with you, for they will surely turn your heart away after their gods." Solomon held fast to these in love. He had seven hundred wives, princesses, and three hundred concubines, and his wives turned his heart away. For when Solomon was old, his wives turned his heart away after other gods; and his heart was not wholly devoted to the LORD his God, as the heart of David his father had been.
>
> —1 KINGS 11:1–4

Solomon ignored his own advice concerning the kinds of people he was to associate with. Proverbs is filled with insights on this subject. His wisdom was never at fault. Nor was his wisdom lacking or weak. But wisdom only benefits those who live by it. Such is the case with this great king. God gave him all the insight needed to keep his throne intact for generations.

> Now the LORD was angry with Solomon because his heart was turned away from the LORD, the God of Israel, who had appeared to him twice, and had commanded him concerning this thing, that he should not go after other gods; but he did not observe what the LORD had commanded.
>
> —1 KINGS 11:9–10

Since you are reading a book about significance, my guess is that you would love to have the opportunities given to Solomon. You and I would almost have to be crazy not to long for the possibilities afforded him. And yet to me the most sobering part of this whole story is the phrase "who had appeared to him twice." God revealed Himself to Solomon in a way that few in all of history can claim. It was extreme favor, yet it was to no avail.

---

Compromise and disobedience never release the kind of favor and increased blessing that will last. *#bornforsignificance*

---

Great experiences come at a cost, as knowledge equals responsibility. Never look at the subtle experiences with God as a negative thing. They are displays of His mercy in that they give us a place to learn to respond to Him. Here we learn of His ways and become completely immersed in responding to His will. Obedience to the subtle becomes the platform for the extreme.

The positive aspect of extreme favor is that great encounters with God give us greater opportunities for breakthrough and increase for our purpose in life. That must be held in tension with the reality that more is required of us as favor increases. Increased revelation of God Himself also creates less room for error.

Moses is a prime example of this truth. He knew God face to face. His encounters are unparalleled in Scripture. And yet God was going to kill him at one point because he hadn't circumcised his sons as he was supposed to do. In other words, along this journey with God are points of obedience for each of us. And while the lack of circumcision seemed to be OK for a certain part of the journey, it was not OK for where God was taking him. Moses repented quickly and did what he was supposed to do.

This sobering reality is not to keep us from seeking God's face. But it is to awaken us to this fact: "From everyone who has been given much, much will be required; and to whom they entrusted much, of him they will ask all the more" (Luke 12:48).

## IN THE GLORY

Solomon certainly had God-given moments that should have convinced him of the correctness of his father's ways. In the dedication of the temple, we see something extraordinary: the glory of God.

> When the priests came forth from the holy place (for all the priests who were present had sanctified themselves, without regard to divisions), and all the Levitical singers, Asaph, Heman, Jeduthun, and their sons and kinsmen, clothed in fine linen, with cymbals, harps and lyres, standing east of the altar, and with them one hundred and twenty priests blowing trumpets in unison when the trumpeters and the singers were to make themselves heard with one voice to praise and to glorify the LORD, and when they lifted up their voice accompanied by trumpets and cymbals and instruments of music, and when they praised the LORD saying, "He indeed is good for His lovingkindness is everlasting," then the house, the house of the LORD, was filled with a cloud, so that the priests could not stand to minister because of the cloud, for *the glory of the Lord filled the house of God.*
>
> —2 CHRONICLES 5:11–14

God doesn't manifest His glory carelessly. He is measured and intentional. I wouldn't want to say that we earn His manifested presence, but neither do I want to imply that God is random or cavalier in His choices. In both Old and New Testaments, the word *presence* means face. When His presence is recognized, His face is present. And it is His face that marks us with favor and blessing.

This moment should have sealed the deal for Solomon regarding what is important in life. There is nothing greater than the presence of God. And to become satisfied with routine instead of a divine encounter is hard to imagine, especially for one who was exposed to the glory of God in response to worship. The fact that the priests couldn't stand to minister was to signify the overwhelming nature of God's presence.

That was the purpose of David's tabernacle: to provide a place of continuous worship where God is glorified and the people of God are exposed to their reason for being alive. Presence. The face of God. Nothing can ever surpass the face of God being turned toward us, as is seen in this beautiful dedication of the temple.

## SOLOMON, THE ULTIMATE CASE STUDY

Solomon's life provides us with enough material to easily fill this entire book on significance. He correctly illustrated the *purpose* of blessing when he prayed for wisdom. He knew his responsibilities were great. He also knew that he didn't have what was needed to care for God's people correctly and viewed himself with true humility. Blessing, promotion, and increase equipped him to serve others on a supernatural level, bringing Israel into a place of significance as never seen before. The measure of influence and impact we are capable of having is unheard of without these grace gifts from God.

He also exhibits the *process* quite well in that he walked in humility, chose well under pressure, and valued his responsibilities over personal gain. For this reason, God gave him all he *could* have asked for but didn't.

When thinking of Solomon, many focus on the *perils* of his promotion. The higher we rise, the more catastrophic our fall. Such is the case with Solomon. He led Israel into their greatest season of significance and influence. He then tragically brought them into bondage that would take multiple generations to remove.

## BLESSINGS INCREASE RESPONSIBILITY

I've read the stories of some of the great revivalists of years past. Their experiences in God and in ministry always move me deeply. I consider them great heroes of the faith. One of the most frequent mistakes made by these great leaders is that when the favor of God is upon them and power is flowing through them in an unprecedented measure, the notion seems to creep in that compromise is acceptable. It seems to start small. But when God's blessing is still on their lives, it gets translated that God is OK with their behavior. It's strange, but some of the greatest times of failure have followed their greatest victories.

---

The blessing of the Lord breeds entitlement in the people of God if they don't remain humble and practice discipline. #bornforsignificance

---

But then isn't that what happened to Elijah? As I mentioned earlier, he boldly faced 850 false prophets on Mount Carmel, displaying God's might and favor, bringing an end to their influence over Israel by having them killed. But in the next scene, he runs and hides because of a rumored threat by a woman, Jezebel. In fact, Elijah's emotional condition was so bad he wanted to die. Even positive emotional experiences can be draining.

The blessing of the Lord breeds *entitlement* in the people of God if they don't remain humble and practice discipline. Those two practices keep the blessing a positive element. As you look through Israel's history, you find times when they came into great extravagance. In Solomon's era, they say silver piled up on the streets. It was too common to bother counting. What does that say about the prosperity of a city, of a nation? The blessing of the Lord upon them in that season was so extreme that they didn't bother counting what was precious to them in other seasons.

---

Blessings are supposed to have one basic effect on how we live and think: they are to draw us to the One who gives the blessing. *#bornforsignificance*

---

Not maintaining that sense of humility and personal discipline gets us into trouble. My personal conviction is that the Lord would pour out blessing on every believer greater than we have the intelligence or imagination to ask for. But He is more concerned with our outcome than how much we enjoy the journey. He's more concerned about what we become inside than what we experience outside. Jesus, without question, prioritizes our inner world. He speaks to the inner world consistently. In fact, He says the kingdom of God is within us.

All kingdom issues are internal, personal, heartfelt issues. Any time we deal with kingdom realities, we deal with them from the heart first. It's why Jesus would come into a situation and say that if you want to be exalted, you have to lower yourself.

Blessings are supposed to have one basic effect on how we live and think: they are to draw us to the One who gives the blessing. In other words, they are to endear us to the One who has displayed such care over our lives. But when they insulate us from the needs of others, make us feel superior in any way, or even give us a special license to sin or compromise, they have been misused. God blesses us because He loves us. But the end game is that the ends of the earth would know what He is like and be drawn to Him. That is the role of divine favor upon all of our lives. It's priceless, powerful, effective—and dangerous if misapplied.

CHAPTER 12

# OUR INNER WORLD

PRAYERS ANOINTED BY the Holy Spirit are very similar in nature to prophecies. They reveal God's intent and purpose. One of my favorites in the whole Bible is the prayer found in 3 John 2: "Beloved, I pray that in all respects you may prosper and be in good health, just as your soul prospers."

It is quite interesting that this anointed prayer reveals the heart of God for each of us. He has not only willed for us to be in good health and to prosper, but He also instructs how. It begs the questions:

- *Why does God give us instructions on how to have a healthy family?* Because He wants us to have a healthy family: spirit, soul, and body.
- *Why does God give us instructions on how to have a healthy thought life?* Because He wants us to have a healthy thought life.
- *So then, why does He give instruction on how to prosper?* The answer is obvious but not religiously acceptable, in part because of abuses. But truth is truth, and it must not be rendered powerless because of another person's abuse. Instead

of ignoring truth because of the risks involved, we must return to humility, thankfulness, and accountability in our relationships so we can discover God's heart in a matter.

I've studied 3 John 2 for so many years, and yet it still amazes me. Our inner world has an effect on our health. I guess we've known that for decades. Doctors have told us that our emotional health, when infected with bitterness, anger, jealousy, and fear, affects our bodies in very destructive ways. So then, that's not new. But what still adds the wow factor to my thinking is that the measure in which my soul prospers affects my finances.

---

Instead of ignoring truth because of the risks, we must return to humility, thankfulness, and accountability in our relationships so we can discover God's heart in a matter. *#bornforsignificance*

---

In one sense, this is logical. For example, a server who is joyful and loves serving people is going to get larger tips. A salesperson with a similar attitude will have more clients, resulting in more commissions. What moves me most about this is that the way a person prospers is not always logical. Whenever we have a victorious internal life, it attracts the favor of God, which is what brings the increase of income. The health of our souls is what has a great effect on our physical and financial health. More specifically, the Bible affirms we are to prosper in *all respects*. This means that in every area of our lives, there must be blessing.

## FAITH IS AN INSIDE JOB

Managing our inner world is central to all matters of faith. Our heart is the seat of affection and the place from which flow the issues that affect our lives. Faith comes from the heart as well, not the mind. Faith is not an idea or a concept. It is not a doctrine to be believed in. Faith is an inward expression of confidence in God being who He says He is and doing what He says He will do.

The most trustworthy One in the universe values being trusted. Faith is the most well-deserved expression we could ever give to God, the perfectly faithful One. It is obviously not to satisfy His ego, as He is the person of love, which never seeks its own. (See 1 Corinthians 13:5.) Our trust in God is an act of justice. Consider this: For the most trustworthy One in the universe to be trusted is an act of justice. Faith is not the result of striving. It is the result of surrender. It is also an expression of holiness. Because we are separated unto Him, we discover His absolute reliability in all things, resulting in great faith. The more we are separated unto Him, the easier the issue of faith becomes.

The Scripture says that without faith it is impossible to please Him. It's not that He is hard to please, in some finicky or angry way. It is simply unjust to do otherwise. Not to believe Him is to deny all that is right with the world, building our lives on the inferior. Anything outside of faith wars against the purposes of God in the earth. To be true to who He is and all that He has purposed to do with those made in His image, it is vital that we believe. It is vital that we are people of great faith, for He is the God of great people.

## JESUS BROUGHT THE NEW

What the Old Testament hinted at, Jesus hit head-on. Instead of using outward signs of blessing as the litmus test of divine favor, Jesus spoke of a superior reality of God's grace working on the inside of a person. Where the Old Testament used wealth and fame as outward signs of divine favor, the New Testament uses internal realities as real evidence. We are changed from the inside out. Much of the church has rejected any sign of outward favor being wrong, and they tragically lack the internal prosperity of soul that is to be the priority of the two. Financial prosperity is not inherently evil, or God would never describe heaven with streets of gold and gates of pearl. Money is not to be served, nor is it the priority of the believer's pursuit. Internal health and even wealth are to be chosen.

Even Proverbs, written by the richest man ever to live, nailed this subject well. Wisdom is to be chosen above riches (16:16). What was seen in form in the Old Testament is clear in the New. It wasn't until we could experience the complete forgiveness of sin and have the indwelling Holy Spirit that it was possible for everyone to become internally wealthy. It is now the norm. At least, it is supposed to be.

## THE SERMON OF SERMONS

The Sermon on the Mount—and especially the Beatitudes—profoundly addresses this topic. Jesus' teaching often overwhelmed listeners. The officers sent out by the Pharisees returned, saying, "No man ever spoke like this Man!" (John 7:46, NKJV).

Two Beatitudes are particularly worth mentioning in this context: "Blessed are the poor in spirit, for theirs is the kingdom of heaven" (Matt. 5:3) and "Blessed are the pure in heart, for they shall see God" (Matt. 5:8). As I mentioned earlier in this book, the word *blessed* is the word *happy*. Happiness belongs to those who are humble and pure. These two traits define the nature of our internal world as priorities of kingdom living.

## MATTERS OF THE HEART

Jesus always addressed the matters of the heart. That's the place from which our lives are lived. It's the basic reason that material things are a poor thermometer for measuring our spirituality.

Biblical management is not restriction in the sense of killing dreams or creativity. It's quite the opposite. True management of the heart is an invitation for purpose and liberty. The laws of God don't restrict us from freedom or from our own unique expression. Each of God's commandments is an invitation to life. He who designed us knows exactly what is needed for us to become all that He intended. His commandments are just that: invitations. Every word invites us further into this relational journey where we know Him more and behold Him more clearly. Perhaps you've read that "when we see Him, we will become like Him" (1 John 3:2). It's true. But it can also be said that "*as* we see Him, we will become like Him."

---

Jesus always addressed the matters of the heart.... It's the basic reason that material things are a poor thermometer for measuring our spirituality. *#bornforsignificance*

---

To fail at managing our inner world but instead work at managing our outward behavior only is an invitation for disaster. All the issues of life flow from our inner man. Seeing this clearly is what helps us to prioritize what's important to Him. Jesus warns of the kinds of things that come from the heart of a person, and it is sobering indeed.

> But the things that proceed out of the mouth come from the heart, and those defile the man. For out of the heart come evil thoughts, murders, adulteries, fornications, thefts, false witness, slanders. These are the things which defile the man; but to eat with unwashed hands does not defile the man.
>
> —Matthew 15:18–20

Many of the things we dislike about our lives were first put into place through carelessness in our speech. And while you may be able to find abuses to this principle on the power of our words through confession, the fact remains the same: "Death and life are in the power of the tongue." That is the Bible—Proverbs 18:21, to be exact. Many who attack the issues of confession and faith have undermined their own invitation to know and become like the Son of God, Jesus Christ, whose words were spirit and life. (See John 6:63.)

We are disciples of Jesus. He said what the Father was saying. We have access to that same reality and can say what is in the heart of our heavenly Father at any given moment. But when our speech contradicts what He is saying, regardless of how spiritual it sounds to our friends, it is foolish. And there's not one of us who enjoys harvesting from the seeds planted in those times. The mind focused on the flesh brings death and is incapable of obeying what God is saying. Such harmful speech reveals where the mind has set its focus. (See Romans 8:6–8.) And whether you care to accept it or not, that carnal focus is at war with God.

---

Many of the things we dislike about our lives were first put into place through carelessness in our speech. *#bornforsignificance*

---

I find it alarming that so many speak negatively and think God is OK with it. Just because some abuse this principle for selfish gain doesn't legitimize the neglect of truth. The abuse of a principle never legitimizes the neglect of that principle.

Each word Jesus speaks becomes spirit and life. Think of it: Words become spirit; they become presence. And that presence gives life. That's the nature of His voice to us. It breathes life into the soul of the listener. When we partner with the Father as Jesus exemplified, we too bring life into dead situations.

## INSIDE OUT

Our internal reality becomes our external reality. That is the nature of life for the believer. Inside first, which means the thoughts, ambitions, and desires that are shaped by His heart will eventually influence and help design the nature of the world we will live in.

Jesus slept in a storm, which shows He had great peace. But when He stood to confront the storm by rebuking it and then declaring peace, the storm stopped. It was no match for the peace that was in Him. His internal reality became His external reality.

> Then He arose and rebuked the wind, and said to the sea, "Peace, be still!" And the wind ceased and there was a great calm.
>
> —Mark 4:39, NKJV

These stories are more than entertainment. They are patterns for life. They illustrate what the renewed mind looks like in a practical sense.

The Bible is the anchor of the heart and mind—the plumb line. The standard set in the Scriptures is what introduces us to the grace that makes living like Jesus, inside and out, even possible. The more our inner world reflects His heart, the more we can be trusted to influence the world around us.

The pure in heart will see God. Purity in our inner man enables us to see what otherwise would be missed: God Himself. He can be found by those whose hearts are pure. Grace empowers us to perform His will. Law requires; grace enables.

---

One of the biggest challenges in ministry is to give yourself to a people group, to an assignment, without picking up the offenses of the people you're serving. *#bornforsignificance*

---

Favor usually manifests outwardly. It's recognized by title, resource, authority, and anointing. But what He releases to our outer man is according to what He's found on the inside. We are designed to mirror outwardly what's happening behind the scenes in our private life. A verse quoted before in this book is Proverbs 4:23: "Watch over your heart with all diligence, for from it flow the issues of life." Jesus said in Luke 17:21, "The kingdom of God is within you" (NKJV), which to me means all kingdom issues are matters of the heart. And while I may not understand all the implications of these statements, I know for certain that my priority is to manage my inner world well.

## LIVING UNOFFENDED

One of the biggest challenges in ministry is to give yourself to a people group, to an assignment, without picking up the offenses of the people you're serving. Can you minister to children without being offended at the adults who don't prioritize children? Can you minister to adults without being offended at young people who show no respect to adults? Can you serve the poor without being offended at the rich? Can you serve the rich without being offended at those who won't work? Can you minister to one race without being offended at another race? Can you serve prisoners without becoming angry at those who seek justice? These are very real and challenging situations.

I've watched this for years and have watched people give themselves in ministry to their assignment. The mistake is made when we feel the need to prove our solidarity with that group, and we ignorantly pick up their offenses. It masquerades as a partnership of sorts. It is possible to feel someone's pain without picking up their spiritual disease.

I'm sure many would call that offense bitterness. Bitterness in any measure is contaminating in nature. A warning given in Hebrews 12:15 is that bitterness causes trouble, defiling many. I think one of the main things that keeps us from having the cultural impact that God has assigned for us is the challenge of wading deep into the dark places of life and serving well without getting contaminated by the sins people carry. James put it this way:

> But if you have bitter envy and self-seeking in your hearts, do not boast and lie against the truth. *This wisdom* does not descend from above, but is earthly, sensual, demonic.

> For where envy and self-seeking exist, confusion and every evil thing are there.
>
> —James 3:14–16, NKJV

What did he just say? Bitterness and self-promotion masquerade as wisdom. James writes, "*This wisdom* does not descend from above, but is earthly, sensual, demonic." Did you see it? "This wisdom...." Bitterness and offense appeal to our reason as they satisfy our need for justice. They give the holder a sense of correctness. I have yet to meet a bitter person who didn't have a good reason. But it is inferior reasoning.

If you carry offense in your heart toward somebody, you will also attract the information and the people of like mind who are needed to reinforce the offense. It is the unseen law of attraction. People will always reinforce what you truly value in your heart of hearts, whether it's good or bad. The root of this is boasting, in other words, pride. Pride attracts reasons for resentment. It also inspires a person to lie against the truth and call it truth.

The most dangerous part of this trap is that it credits the sin of bitterness with the spiritual gift of discernment. Anytime we take dysfunction and call it by a spiritual name, we give it permission to stay and grow. It remains until it sets roots down into our personalities. What starts as a sin of the flesh becomes a spiritual sin, empowered by the demonic.

Staying clean in attitude is everything. *Everything*. Maintaining humility of heart and mind is essential to the overall health of the individual. This is being healthy on the inside first. It is worth all efforts.

Perhaps it's for this reason Proverbs 4:23 says, "Watch over your heart with all diligence." It's been a life verse for me for forty-some years. Why? Because from it flow the issues of life.

If you could imagine for a moment the heart of a person and from that heart flowing many streams. One stream is family life, while another is mental health, and yet another is finances, and so on. The issues of life flow from this place that I'm to watch over.

The slightest offense, the slightest irritation has to be quickly dealt with. It contaminates all the streams flowing from our lives that are supposed to become rivers of life for the nations. No wonder the enemy of our souls works so hard to contaminate our inner world with such poison.

If you or I innocently accept an inferior thought and dwell on it, after about three or four minutes, roots are starting to set themselves down because the thought that started innocently turned into a reaction of offense.

---

Anytime we take dysfunction and call it by a spiritual name, we give it permission to stay and grow.... What starts as a sin of the flesh becomes a spiritual sin, empowered by the demonic. *#bornforsignificance*

---

Then the roots settle into our personhood. The longer you or I dwell on an offense, the deeper the roots go until they eventually affect our personality. They actually shape the way we think and perceive reality. That's why the Bible says, "Do not let the sun go down on your anger" (Eph. 4:26). Don't go to bed mad. Deal with it before then because if you go to sleep, that thing will foul and fester, and you will have an infection deeply rooted in your heart that you are no longer even aware of. That's where people go through traumatic experiences sometimes with the Lord, just getting free from things they've carried for years. They never knew. They just squashed it down and hid it, not realizing that it became something that was really poisoning their heart. Typically we call this living in denial. Real faith doesn't deny a problem's existence. It just denies the problem a place of influence. Learning to keep ourselves healthy on the inside is vital to our faith.

For me, my inner world stays healthy by my open and transparent relationship with the Lord. Things are kept healthy through confession of sin, wrong attitudes, or even times when it feels like God didn't keep His promise. I never accuse Him, as I know He is perfectly faithful and true. It's impossible for Him to lie. But I will say, "God, I know it's impossible for You to forsake me or lie to me. But I really need Your help, because it feels like You did." I then turn to the Scriptures and read until He heals and fills my soul.

It is my responsibility to manage my inner world. The task does not fall on the shoulders of another. The Holy Spirit is ready, able, and present that I might succeed in this endeavor.

CHAPTER 13

# WHEN REFORMERS FORGET

I LOVE REFORMERS. THESE people courageously live by the principles forgotten by the masses. Their resolve enables them to withstand opposition and push into the promises of God that everybody wants but few are willing to pay the price to obtain. They live with great risk so that a future generation will know what it is to live in the favor and blessing of the Lord. They are multigenerational if they are anything at all.

It needs to be emphasized that these people are the rarest of all of our heroes of the faith, in that they have targeted culture itself. It is not good enough for them that their church or parish succeeds in having many converts. It's not good enough that they have great influence throughout the church. While those things would be the great prize for many leaders throughout history, this rare breed cannot remain quiet until the culture itself changes to accommodate what God has intended to do on planet earth.

They live with the basic conviction that there are biblical answers to every societal problem and challenge. They have the burning conviction that there is more and that their children and grandchildren should be the ones who inherit what God is doing. And while this quote by one of the founding fathers of the USA might seem misplaced to some, it illustrates something of a progression in thought, influence, and liberties found in a developed society.

> I must study politics and war, that our sons may have liberty to study mathematics and philosophy. Our sons ought to study mathematics and philosophy, geography, natural history and naval architecture, navigation, commerce and agriculture in order to give their children a right to study painting, poetry, music, architecture, statuary, tapestry and porcelain.[1]
>
> —John Adams, Letters of John Adams, Addressed to His Wife

I love the wisdom of those words. It reveals the often forgotten reality that a breakthrough in one generation creates an inheritance and momentum for the next. One generation deals with the harder things in life so that preparations can be made for the next generation to build upon their accomplishments. Added to that is the thought that two generations away can have the freedom to explore creativity and artistic expression not afforded those who went before them. It's a beloved quote for me personally because of its understanding of the layers in culture and its reach in vision for future generations.

## FAVORITES

I guess I could say that, for me, any true reformer is a favorite historical figure. They are so few and far between. I love their passion for believing for more than what is typical. In doing so, they often eclipse the impact of other great spiritual leaders. That's what reformers do. But I must admit to having two that stand out for me. The first is Hans Nielsen Hauge,[2] a Norwegian reformer who was a revivalist, an entrepreneur, a businessman, and a true reformer. He was horribly misunderstood and abused by his government as he preached without a license, dying in his fifties from the ill health contracted in his prison life. His mark on Norway remains to this day. And the second is Hezekiah, a noted king in Judah's history. It's the latter of the two I want to speak of in this chapter.

## BEGINNING IN DARKNESS

Hezekiah is often overlooked as a reformer, perhaps because he lived in the days of the Old Testament, yet in some ways, he may be the greatest of all the reformers we could list. His upbringing was a nightmare. He inherited the throne from his dad, a demented spiritual madman. Seeing where he started and the challenges that were before him in his own household, we are able to better appreciate the task ahead for this young man during his growing-up years.

---

A breakthrough in one generation creates an inheritance and momentum for the next. *#bornforsignificance*

---

Hezekiah's father, Ahaz, was a very evil man, an idol-worshiper who decimated the temple of God in Jerusalem before he closed its doors as a place for worshipping the one true God. He also did the unthinkable in sacrificing some of his own children to false gods. Hezekiah was a survivor of such atrocities.

Giving such an offering to idols was thought to increase that person's power in life. Of course, we know it has the opposite effect. Whenever people worship false gods, they always lose a bit of themselves in the process. The psalmist describes the idols and their worshipers, "They have eyes, but they cannot see.... Those who make them will become like them, everyone who trusts in them" (Psalm 115:5, 8). Worshipping false gods makes us like the god being worshipped: they can't see, speak, touch, or hear, and we become like them, losing our humanness in the act of giving ourselves to the inferior in worship. The same is true today whenever we fall into idolatry, which is summed up with the word *greed*. (See Colossians 3:5.)

It's amazing to think that anyone being raised in that atmosphere could come out sane, let alone a great leader. But that is exactly what happened. God used Hezekiah to restore the spiritual life of Judah as a nation, describing him as being like his father, David. Ahaz was his natural father, but his heart and behavior connected him to David, who lived almost three hundred years before him.

David became the standard by which every king was measured. In this interesting verse, we see the prophetic significance of David's life: "the one who is feeble among them in that day will be like David, and the house of David will be like God" (Zech. 12:8). What an unusual comparison of a person's greatness in this prophetic promise.

Being compared to David was the greatest compliment a king could receive from God.

> Hezekiah became king when he was twenty-five years old; and he reigned twenty-nine years in Jerusalem. And his mother's name was Abijah, the daughter of Zechariah. He did right in the sight of the Lord, according to all that his father David had done.
>
> —2 Chronicles 29:1–2

It's a beautiful statement: "He did right in the sight of the Lord." This is what David was known for. He had a heart for God's heart, which meant he valued what God thought and felt. It's beautiful. And now Hezekiah, the man with an occultist upbringing, was about to lead the charge for societal reform. And once again, he did so by returning the values taught and practiced by his father, David.

## FIRST THINGS FIRST

The people of God had fallen into idolatrous worship under Ahaz. It was common for them to be influenced by surrounding nations whenever they forfeited the responsibility to be an influence for God's sake.

It's important for us to remember, we're not merely talking about unusual religious practices. The people of God were involved in things that attract the demonic realm into their lives in a very dark and oppressive nature. The sacrifices alone would invite the devil into places of great influence throughout society, where he could kill, steal, and destroy. Hezekiah took the throne in this most perilous time.

His first assignment was to destroy the worship of false gods that his father had instituted. He tore down the idols and false gods and abolished the worship on the high places that not even Solomon had dealt with. Hezekiah purged the land of these demonic practices, restoring their responsibility of sacrificing to God alone. It wouldn't be a stretch to say that he faced opposition in his reforms. But his gaze was locked into his divine purpose. Nothing would sway him from his moment. In 2 Chronicles 29:11, we read the exhortation to his people.

> My sons, do not be negligent now, for the Lord has chosen you to stand before Him, to minister to Him, and to be His ministers and burn incense.

This word was given to priests. The significance of this moment is once again linked to David and the life he modeled that even was to have an effect on the church age. Hezekiah was leading reform by driving out the evil of the worship of false gods and replacing it with the worship King David instituted during his reign. This is more significant than most of us realize.

When God was leading Ezra and Nehemiah into the rebuilding of the city of Jerusalem, they started by rebuilding the temple. Deciding what or who we will worship determines what we will build. We always become like whatever we worship. This is central to all reform.

## DAVID'S REFORM

Nathan and Gad were prophets who served King David. But Acts 2:29–31 says David himself was also a prophet: "David…was a prophet and…he looked ahead and spoke." This would be very significant, as they were about to get a direction from God that made no sense and, even more challenging, was contrary to the Law they lived under. This direction had to do with worship.

---

Deciding what or who we will worship determines what we will build. We always become like whatever we worship. *#bornforsignificance*

---

This part of David's story is important in this chapter because this is what Hezekiah later restored to Israel. Here's a bit more of the story: Nathan and Gad confirmed what David no doubt learned while on the back side of the desert caring for his father's sheep. God isn't looking for the blood of bulls and goats, but He is looking for the sacrifice that comes from a heart of surrender.

> The sacrifices of God are a broken spirit; a broken and a contrite heart, O God, You will not despise.

—Psalm 51:17

Their prophetic role was also very significant in this journey, and God undoubtedly used them to confirm what David had been sensing, which we'll look at further in the story.

What David brought about in his day was contrary to everything they had previously learned about their approach to God. The ark of the covenant was the place where God's presence rested for the nation of Israel. Priests were never allowed to come before the ark, except the high priest on the Day of Atonement. One day a year. That's it.

When David became king, he picked up the heart of God on the matter. The priests came before the ark, the actual presence of God, twenty-four hours a day, seven days a week. It was a continuous, ongoing ministry to God Himself. This was done with musical instruments and choirs. When you consider that God inhabits the praises of His people, you see how this completely changed the atmosphere of Jerusalem. The manifest presence of God no doubt impacted the people of Jerusalem in profound ways.

When we consider the effect of the presence of the Spirit of God upon David's predecessor, the evil King Saul, we catch a glimpse of what was possible. Saul was hunting down David in order to kill him. He wandered into a group of prophets when the presence of God so overwhelmed him that he prophesied with the accuracy of a seasoned prophet. Under David's rule, Israel was becoming a presence-based land, with a presence-based culture.

Tragically, Solomon, who followed his father David in being king over Israel, never really understood why David was a successful king. The continuous worship and intercession that happened in the place called the tabernacle of David, built on Mount Zion, was no doubt the greatest influence in the nation during David's reign. This kind of ministry to God ended in Solomon's day.

Interestingly enough, in Amos 9, the Old Testament prophet foretold that God would rebuild the tabernacle of David in the last days, which James quoted in Acts 15:16. James used that verse to announce the time is now. And yet, there would be a restoration of that ministry long before the last days began. Hezekiah caught the vision for this.

## HEZEKIAH REBUILDS

Somehow Hezekiah heard about the accomplishments of David, and the Lord gave him insight as to the reason for David's success. His reckless abandon in worship marked Israel forever. When Hezekiah became king, he worked to restore his nation to its place of historical strength by returning to the standard that David had set.

His first task was to get the priests ready for their assignment in life.

> They assembled their brothers, consecrated themselves, and went in to cleanse the house of the Lord, according to the commandment of the king by the words of the Lord.
>
> —2 Chronicles 29:15

After many years of neglect and abuse from the unholy activities of the previous king, the house of God had to be cleansed and restored. Hezekiah followed this with setting the direction for these priests.

> He then stationed the Levites in the house of the Lord with cymbals, with harps and with lyres, according to the command of David and of Gad the king's seer, and of

> Nathan the prophet; for the command was from the Lord through His prophets.
>
> —2 Chronicles 29:25

This passage reveals the worship priority, but also the role that Nathan and Gad played in the decision. It was essential to have godly counsel in the matter, as they were following God off the map. No one had done this before. Ever. And now they were going to approach the ark of God with song. Any improper treatment of the ark brought about death, so this was no small matter. And now Hezekiah was to embark on the same journey.

## GOD BRAGS ON HEZEKIAH!

Let's be honest. We are all living for that moment when we hear, "Well done, good and faithful servant." To have recognition and praise from God is absolutely priceless. Jesus did that a number of times, bragging on people's extraordinary faith. But here God highlights the great impact of this reformer.

> He did right in the sight of the Lord, according to all that his father David had done. He removed the high places and broke down the sacred pillars and cut down the Asherah. He also broke in pieces the bronze serpent that Moses had made, for until those days the sons of Israel burned incense to it; and it was called Nehushtan. He trusted in the Lord, the God of Israel; so that after him there was none like him among all the kings of Judah, nor among those who were before him. For he clung to the Lord; he did not depart from following Him, but kept His commandments, which the Lord had commanded Moses. And the Lord was with him; wherever he went he prospered. And he rebelled against the king of Assyria and did not serve him.
>
> —2 Kings 18:3–7

First of all, Hezekiah is compared to David, whose reign was the high point in Israel's history. Secondly, he tore down the high places, which not even Solomon accomplished. He took it to another level by destroying the worship of false gods. He tore down their altars. He destroyed the bronze serpent of Moses. This is interesting because it was a God-given moment when Moses made what he was instructed by God to make. But the people of God began to worship the tool that God used to bring healing, instead of the God who brought healing. No artifact is deserving of worship. It had to go.

Following the descriptions of what he destroyed, he behaved in a most significant manner. It says Hezekiah trusted in the Lord, he clung to the Lord, and he didn't cease following the Lord. This really is amazing.

---

It is possible to impact God's heart so deeply that favor and protection are given to a generation you will never see. *#bornforsignificance*

---

When the priorities are taken care of, God takes care of the rest. This principle is similar to Matthew 6:33, "Seek first His kingdom... and all these things will be added to you." Whenever we attend to the things that matter to God, He attends to the things that matter to us. It's a beautiful partnership.

The beginning of the last verse in this passage is worth it all. "The Lord was with him." The result of the priority of God's presence is what caused Hezekiah to prosper.

As a result, God declared that there had never been anyone as great as Hezekiah! Did that include David and Solomon? I don't know. But what I do know is that God was moved by this king's choices and priorities. He then marked this man with His presence.

## CHALLENGES COME

Following this great season of blessing and increase, problems arose. During this time, they had threats from surrounding nations and their leaders, with threats of war unto annihilation. Here we see that King Hezekiah learned to pray.

> Then Isaiah the son of Amoz sent to Hezekiah saying, "Thus says the Lord, the God of Israel, 'Because you have prayed to Me about Sennacherib king of Assyria, I have heard you.'"
>
> —2 Kings 19:20

The Lord was moved by his prayers and caused his enemies to destroy themselves. Then He gave him His reasoning: "For I will defend this city to save it for My own sake and for My servant David's sake" (2 Kings 19:34).

Do you see it? It's the influence of King David from hundreds of years earlier. God is going to protect them for His own sake and David's. It's a powerful thought to see that God's sake and David's sake run parallel roads. God considered them one and the same. Here's what moves me so profoundly: it is possible to impact God's heart so deeply that favor and protection are given to a generation you will never see. It is amazing to think that each of us can have this kind of impact on the heart of God. David set the highwater mark for all of us in these matters.

## CHALLENGES INCREASE

Hezekiah became sick and was about to die. In fact, the prophet Isaiah came to see him, instructing him that it was time to get his affairs in order as he was going to die. Hezekiah learned how to pray during times when they were threatened with war and destruction. He turned his heart toward the Lord again.

> "Remember now, O Lord, I beseech You, how I have walked before You in truth and with a whole heart and have done what is good in Your sight." And Hezekiah wept bitterly.
>
> —2 Kings 20:3

I love prayers where the people of God remind God of their obedience. You can only do that when you have relational equity, and you're confident of God's heart to respond. It's not that God forgets. Never. But this kind of praying is good for us because it puts us in line with God's heart and causes us to remember and declare the reality of a covenant with God. It is a humbling thing for us to remind God of our obedience. It positions us in a place of abandonment with expectation.

Before Isaiah made it out of the courtyard of the palace, God spoke again, promising Hezekiah fifteen more years. Isaiah returned to give him the good news.

> I will add fifteen years to your life, and I will deliver you and this city from the hand of the king of Assyria; and I will defend this city for My own sake and for My servant David's sake.
>
> —2 Kings 20:6

Notice, again, there is another breakthrough for Hezekiah and his family for God's sake and for David's.

## PERSONAL FRUSTRATION

Here is where I have issues with many who teach on this story. It is well known that Hezekiah has some major problems following this moment in his life. We'll look at why in a minute. My problem is with those who say, "Hezekiah should never have asked for God to spare his life. He should have settled for God's will."

This is irritating because responding to God in prayer when problems or challenges come *is* God's will. That is how He designed us all: to pray! That logic makes me never want to pray because, who knows, maybe I'll pray for something God doesn't want, and I'll fail as a result. That takes the wind out of my sail quite quickly.

Prayer is His idea. And I am comforted knowing that God always reserves the right not to answer any prayer that undermines my purpose in life. He is God, knowing the beginning from the end, and always has my best interest in mind.

He answered Hezekiah's prayer because Hezekiah prayed. Period. Hezekiah laid it all on the line with passionate prayers, and it moved the heart of God to act on his behalf. It's beautiful. But what Hezekiah does with this moment is entirely up to him.

## THE DOWNFALL BEGINS

Hezekiah's recovery from sickness became well known, as did his prosperity and fame. The surrounding nations knew God had defended him from their enemies, and there was a certain awe associated with his name. His blessed life was a sign of God's favor. But it created an appetite that worked against his purpose for being.

> Hezekiah had very great riches and honor. And he made himself treasuries for silver, for gold, for precious stones, for spices, for shields, and for all kinds of desirable items; storehouses for the harvest of grain, wine, and oil;

> and stalls for all kinds of livestock, and folds for flocks. Moreover he provided cities for himself, and possessions of flocks and herds in abundance; for God had given him very much property. This same Hezekiah also stopped the water outlet of Upper Gihon, and brought the water by tunnel to the west side of the City of David. Hezekiah prospered in all his works.
>
> However, regarding the ambassadors of the princes of Babylon, whom they sent to him to inquire about the wonder that was done in the land, God withdrew from him, in order to test him, that He might know all that was in his heart.
>
> —2 Chronicles 32:27–31, nkjv

It's a scary thing to be left alone. But with God, it's never punishment. God doesn't give us the silent treatment as people do to one another. Usually, when He is silent, it is because He has already spoken, and it's up to us to find what has been said. When God is silent, He is giving us the opportunity to remember what He has already taught us, so we live from the principles gained during that season.

Theologically, we know that God will never leave us or forsake us. That is His covenantal promise. But it is also true that there are times when the "felt presence" of God is gone. In those moments or seasons, He seems to shut down our capacity to perceive Him. Living consciously aware of God is the great pleasure of life.

---

When God is silent, He is giving us the opportunity to remember what He has already taught us, so we live from the principles gained during that season. *#bornforsignificance*

---

A sobering part of church history is that we can look at the lives of person after person who did stunningly well when the Spirit of God was on them. They were involved in great exploits, great miracles, and bold faith. But these same people often crashed when the Spirit of God lifted.

This was Hezekiah's moment to prove that what was in his heart at his highest point in life was still in him in this moment of testing. The visit from Babylonian leaders is an interesting part of the story, revealing a crack in the king's foundation that had not surfaced before. They came to bring him gifts after hearing that he had been sick. I'm not sure if they were ill-intentioned when they came for a visit. It may have been a goodwill gesture.

> And many were bringing gifts to the Lord at Jerusalem and choice presents to Hezekiah king of Judah, so that he was exalted in the sight of all nations thereafter.
>
> —2 Chronicles 32:23

Hezekiah was now more and more in the spotlight, becoming the target of gifts, blessings, praises, and much international attention. The one who was the target of military assaults and much scorn among the nations was now the media darling, to use a modern term. Something both wonderful and scary happened. Hezekiah had learned to live righteously under pressure and scorn. Now he would have to manage his heart during the times of favor and increase.

> Hezekiah listened to them, and showed them all his treasure house, the silver and the gold and the spices and the precious oil and the house of his armor and all that was found in his treasuries. There was nothing in his house nor in all his dominion that Hezekiah did not show them.
>
> —2 Kings 20:13

The king was moved by all this attention, so much so that he showed them everything he owned. The need to obtain favor from people, especially outsiders, is a potential weakness that Solomon had modeled before him. This didn't serve as the warning to Hezekiah that it should have. He was now doing the same thing, although it manifested differently. He wanted to appear blessed and powerful to the leaders of other nations when, in reality, he already was. We lose so much when we fight to obtain what we already have.

This insecurity is the beginning of a downward spiral from which it is tough to recover. Something as simple as the need to be well thought of, often by people who don't matter, becomes the breaking point. Hezekiah wanted the respect of Babylon, of all places. Whenever God exposes our insecurity, He is doing us a favor. As I mentioned earlier, insecurity is wrong security exposed.

---

We lose so much when we fight to obtain what we already have. *#bornforsignificance*

---

It is easy to think that favor from unbelievers is a primary goal for the Christian. It is, but only when God is giving it, not when it's ours to obtain. Favor is a wonderful gift when it comes from our living in the lordship of Jesus. But when favor is obtained by compromise, it will be sustained only by compromise. This creates a weakening of character that is catastrophic in nature, ultimately destroying any trace of divine favor for a secular setting. It's vital for us to remember that favor comes from the Lord. Let me put it another way: The only favor worth having is the favor given to us by God as we thrive in the lordship of Jesus. It is His gift to us.

Consider this: Hezekiah was strong in battle. He was strong in bringing reform, regardless of the opposition. He sought God in the midst of a national disaster as well as when he was assaulted with personal sickness. He was known to pray effectively at the right moment and in the right way.

Learning to pray with passion is much easier when we're in pain or conflict. Passionate prayers make the greatest difference in our lives. If a prayer doesn't move me, it's not likely to move Him. But if we know to pray with passion only when we're in trial, we'll pray effectively only in the midst of problems. The challenge is to go beyond that and learn to pray passionately because of hope!

The apostle Paul taught us this lesson quite well.

> I know how to get along with humble means, and I also know how to live in prosperity; in any and every circumstance I have learned the secret of being filled and going hungry, both of having abundance and suffering need. I can do all things through Him who strengthens me.
>
> —Philippians 4:12–13

The lesson seems clear to me. "I can do all things…" refers both to times of plenty and of want. Paul needed the same strength in his life when he was in the season of abundance as when he was in great need. This has been the challenge for centuries. How can we be blessed and still remain dependent on God? If we don't learn this, our influence is limited. If we can learn it well, we will be given access to the part of the Great Commission often thought to be out of reach: discipling nations. Only blessed people can succeed in that assignment.

## THE TEST

This is a moment of testing. Sometimes the test isn't difficult, in the sense that it is problem- or crisis-centered. I said earlier that tests are easier when we know we are being tested. Put another way, our greatest tests come when we don't know we're being tested. In this case, success is the greater trial. The test is to see what measure of glory we can live with.

At this point, you might be thinking, "But Bill, God will not give His glory to another." And that's true. But we're not *another*. We are members of His body, created for glory. And that is the problem with sin. The Bible says, "For all have sinned and fall short of the glory of God" (Rom. 3:23). Glory was the original target that we fell short of because of sin. The blood of Jesus restores us to His original intent: living in the glory. The goal is not for *us* to be glorified. That would be a horrible perversion of His design and purpose. The goal is for us to live in His glory in such a way that God Himself is exalted all the more.

If the foundations of our lives have fractures, they become obvious and begin to crumble under the weighty increase of blessing and glory. This is why we are warned not to release certain responsibilities to new believers. They'll fall under the weight. Seasoned people handle the weightier parts of life with grace and stability. The right amount is what we carry responsibly for His glory. That measure doesn't crush us; it establishes us.

To succeed in these seasons, Hezekiah would have to live from the things he learned in the fire of difficulty. The lessons learned in the problems of life are the ones to be remembered for the blessings of life. So what did he learn? He learned obedience. He learned to pray with complete abandonment to God. These are the things that could take him into greater glory.

He had been thoroughly trained for this moment of blessing. Exaltation is often the reward for living in humility. Oftentimes, trusting God regardless of circumstances is what proves our humility. Hezekiah had already succeeded with these issues in the past, but he would have to do it again by remembering his *why*. He would have to remember what got him to where he was.

---

The lessons learned in the problems of life are the ones to be remembered for the blessings of life. *#bornforsignificance*

---

## THE OPPOSITE OF A REFORMER

A leadership team from Babylon came with gifts to visit Hezekiah. Because he wanted to impress these from another land, he showed them everything he owned. He left nothing out. Showing restraint, especially when you're with people you have no relationship with, is the way of wisdom in kingdom thinking. Flaunting blessing to obtain greater favor undermines our purpose. Hezekiah traded his place of security with God for security in the opinions of others. The fear of man is at the root of endless problems for us all.

> Then Isaiah the prophet came to King Hezekiah and said to him, "What did these men say, and from where have they come to you?" And Hezekiah said, "They have come from a far country, from Babylon." He said, "What have they seen in your house?" So Hezekiah answered, "They have seen all that is in my house; there is nothing among my treasuries that I have not shown them."
>
> —2 Kings 20:14–15

It still wasn't clicking. "From a far country" was to make the twinge of guilt seem less important than it was. In other words, we know from these words to the prophet that he knew better. When we exaggerate descriptions to make things appear better than they are, we are practicing subtle dishonesty. Seeds are planted in these moments that we will have to harvest. And it won't be fun.

> Then Isaiah said to Hezekiah, "Hear the word of the LORD. 'Behold, the days are coming when all that is in your house, and all that your fathers have laid up in store to this day will be carried to Babylon; nothing shall be left,' says the LORD.
>
> 'Some of your sons who shall issue from you, whom you will beget, will be taken away; and they will become officials in the palace of the king of Babylon.'"
>
> —2 KINGS 20:16–18

In other words, when you compromise to obtain favor, you lose the favor you had. What was the Lord looking for from this king? He was looking for a king who would pray just like he did when faced with sickness and threats of annihilation through war.

The Bible calls this prayer posture standing in the gap (Ezek. 22:30). It describes taking a position of protection for others in our prayers. God was looking for Hezekiah to take the word of judgment to heart and cry out for mercy. He already had a history with God and knew what He was like. But instead of living like a reformer, living for the sake of a generation to come, he responded in an unthinkable way.

> So Hezekiah said to Isaiah, "The word of the LORD which you have spoken is good!" For he said, "Will there not be peace and truth at least in my days?"
>
> —2 KINGS 20:19, NKJV

The response of this hero of the faith is insane. Literally. How does the father of a reformation movement lose track of his purpose to the extent that he is OK with causing an entire generation to suffer for his bad choices? It's as though the Lord is saying, "What you've done in flaunting blessing to obtain illegitimate favor will cost the descendants after you." And Hezekiah's response is the worst part of the story: "At least there will be peace in my days." How is it even possible, even for a bad father, to be OK with his children being sold into slavery and made eunuchs, which is obviously their suffering for his bad choices? And it was OK with him? It's crazy how blind our own pride can make us. As the Scripture states, "Pride goes before destruction" (Prov. 16:18). The evidence of that truth is clear with this formerly great king.

---

When you compromise to obtain favor, you lose the favor you had. *#bornforsignificance*

---

The Lord is looking for a father who will maintain his priestly responsibility by saying, "God, not on my kids. They didn't sin against You, and they don't deserve this. It was me. It was my pride. Please forgive me and show mercy to my children." Instead, we have a man who is unmoved by the word that his children will be taken captive by the same group that saw his treasures.

There's a time and place for transparency, and this wasn't it. It's never a tool to impress others. Hezekiah became so calloused by his need for recognition that he missed his moment to pray. He already knew of God's mercy in such times. He had a well-respected history with God in this area. But pride robs the heart of passion for God, pure and simple. Pride is truly a thief.

## THE ROOT PROBLEM

Hezekiah was known for rebuilding a lifestyle of worship for the nation and especially for the priests of the Lord. David set the pattern. But Hezekiah failed at maintaining his personal involvement in the same way David did. I'm sure he still gave sacrifices to God and continued the routine of worship. But it was no longer the kind of expression that cost him.

> But Hezekiah gave no return for the benefit he received, because his heart was proud.
>
> —2 Chronicles 32:25

There it is. This is what brought about the collapse of this great reformer's life and legacy. *His sacrifices to God did not equal the favor given to Him.* Token obedience eases the conscience but does nothing to transform our lives.

This passage of Scripture shows us how the kingdom of this great king began to crumble. He lost the position to set up Judah for a measure of reformation they had never experienced before. It would have been multigenerational. But He lost the position to prepare the next generation when he stopped increasing the measure of sacrifice that was equal to the measure of favor and blessing.

Sacrifice is an essential part of our life with God, even in the New Testament. Of course, Jesus is the ultimate sacrifice, made for us to have salvation now and a future forever. Yet it remains an important part of life. I don't care if it's financial giving to the church or the poor. It doesn't matter to me if it's giving thanksgiving and praise to God with shouting and dancing.

What was difficult yesterday has become normal today. What was sacrificial yesterday becomes commonplace today. The challenge is when we become satisfied in a routine and we lose the heart. Remember, David taught us that the sacrifice God is looking for is from the yielded heart. That's the point. When we quit breaking new ground, we have the tendency to stop giving God that which costs us something.

---

Token obedience eases the conscience but does nothing to transform our lives. *#bornforsignificance*

---

God compared Hezekiah to David, but in Hezekiah's moment of crisis, he crashed. In David's moment of crisis, he said, "I'm not going to give to God something that didn't cost me anything." In David's moment, he increased the sacrifice, and he increased the offering. He laid his heart on the line.

God has no need of my sacrifices whatsoever. The dead sheep offered in David's day did nothing for Him. The money we give today is unneeded by Him completely. Sacrifices are not for Him, in the sense that they bring Him any benefit. Giving in the way we were designed to do is what keeps *us* healthy. To respond in an inadequate way affects our health, inside and out. For us to withhold offerings is to rob ourselves of the future He intended for us.

This reveals a vital part of life that is often overlooked: our response to Him must mirror His response to us. He considers me the pearl of great price. I, in turn, must view Him as the pearl of great price for me. I am the apple of His eye. He must then become the focus of my entire life. He gave His life for mine. How can I give Him anything less? My response to Him must be equally significant to the measure of His impact on my life. To give anything less is to withhold what is due Him. It is robbery. This sounds like a hard mandate, much like the requirements of the Law. It's not. At least it's not when you're in love. The whole issue of maintaining a first-love relationship with Jesus is at the core of our design. Anything less is dishonest.

## THE COST OF TOKEN OBEDIENCE

The Book of Proverbs gives us a startling lesson on passion vs. complacency that can help us understand why Hezekiah's choices were so devastating.

> He who is slothful in his work is a brother to him who is a great destroyer.
>
> —PROVERBS 18:9, NKJV

Picture three groups of people for the illustration given in this verse. First are the passionate, faithful workers. Second are the lazy or slothful workers. And finally, there are those who oppose the work. Which two are most alike? The lazy person and the destructive worker are the two most similar. Now picture a passionate servant of the Lord. Then there is a complacent believer, followed by the opponent to the gospel. Which two are most alike? It's frightening to consider, but it's the complacent believer and the opponent to the gospel. In some ways, the life of the complacent legitimizes the opponent to the gospel. And the effect of Hezekiah's life bears witness to this conclusion.

> Manasseh was twelve years old when he became king, and he reigned fifty-five years in Jerusalem. His mother's name was Hephzibah. And he did evil in the sight of the LORD, according to the abominations of the nations whom the LORD had cast out before the children of Israel. For he rebuilt the high places which Hezekiah his father had destroyed; he raised up altars for Baal, and made a wooden image, as Ahab king of Israel had done; and he

> worshiped all the host of heaven and served them. He also built altars in the house of the Lord, of which the Lord had said, "In Jerusalem I will put My name." And he built altars for all the host of heaven in the two courts of the house of the Lord. Also he made his son pass through the fire, practiced soothsaying, used witchcraft, and consulted spiritists and mediums. He did much evil in the sight of the Lord, to provoke Him to anger. He even set a carved image of Asherah that he had made, in the house of which the Lord had said to David and to Solomon his son, "In this house and in Jerusalem, which I have chosen out of all the tribes of Israel, I will put My name forever; and I will not make the feet of Israel wander anymore from the land which I gave their fathers—only if they are careful to do according to all that I have commanded them, and according to all the law that My servant Moses commanded them." But they paid no attention, and Manasseh seduced them to do more evil than the nations whom the Lord had destroyed before the children of Israel.
>
> —2 Kings 21:1–9, nkjv

Manasseh, the son of Hezekiah, was twelve years old when he became king. This means that he was born during the fifteen-year period when God extended his father's life. This should have been the time when Hezekiah's passion for God was at its highest, as God had spared his life and increased his favor on an international level. But it wasn't. Manasseh was born during the years when Hezekiah's sacrifices were token offerings. They didn't illustrate the passion for God he had in the first part of his reign. When young people are born into religious traditions and forms without the manifestation of God's presence and power, there is a much greater likelihood they will choose an alternate way of life. Complacency fuels the heart of the opponent to the gospel.

To describe Manasseh's lifestyle as alternative is being kind. He became the biblical example of corrupt, evil, and demonic. He was worse than the people of the nations God drove out of the Promised Land, which Israel inherited. And that is saying a lot. As great as Hezekiah was in his beginning days, so Manasseh was evil in his beginning. A beautiful part of the story is that, eventually, Manasseh repented. There was enough evidence of truth in his father's traditions that it became *due north* in this thinking when he was in trouble.

---

The need for applause and the desire to impress people with God's favor are signs of weakness that will affect our legacy. *#bornforsignificance*

---

The problem isn't with being blessed. If it were, we could blame God for causing Hezekiah's fall. Blessing is an essential tool that will help us finish our assignments. We are blessed to be a blessing. But favor also puts us into a place where pride becomes an option, should we not maintain humility and trust. This is the path that Hezekiah fell into when his offerings were no longer sacrificial in nature. Instead, his efforts were in building his kingdom and fighting for favor from surrounding nations.

The need for applause and the desire to impress people with God's favor are signs of weakness that will affect our legacy. These values are evidence of the fear of man, which always replaces the fear of God. Whenever God reveals these issues in our lives, it is so we will acknowledge what we need to deal with and truly humble ourselves in the process. Ignoring them only accentuates the weaknesses and increases the impact of our collapse.

Thankfully, the perils of promotion are not automatic. In other words, I'm not saying that failure is the only option when we're blessed. Success is possible—and probable—if we stay humble and dependent on God during the times of blessing in the same measure as in the times of trials.

Departing from our responsibilities and assignments is a temptation during blessings. People often think that the ultimate promotion is into nothingness, but that is not so. While rest is more necessary as the years go by, we were designed to represent Him well in labor. "Let the favor of the Lord our God be upon us; and confirm for us the work of our hands; yes, confirm the work of our hands" (Ps. 90:17).

CHAPTER 14

# RECALIBRATING THE HEART

I AM A FIFTH-GENERATION pastor on my dad's side of the family and fourth on my mom's. My children are sixth- and fifth-generation, respectively, in our positions of ministry. We have an unusual family in that regard. Everyone I can think of is a follower of Jesus. But lest I give the wrong idea of our tribe, we are blessed but very far from perfect. All that is right about us is thanks to God's grace, as God has no grandchildren. Each person must come to Him on his or her own and not think they can have a relationship with God because of who their family is.

I write this having recently finished our Thanksgiving holiday as a family. Every year somewhere between forty and fifty family members gather for a big meal and celebration of God's goodness. It really is fun but also very loud, owing to the huge number of children aged ten and under. Let's just say we don't lack enthusiasm in this gathering. I'm sure the sheer volume of noise has inspired many adults to pray for good weather on this holiday, just so the children can exhaust themselves outside before eating.

My mom is about to turn ninety-one. She is in her element whenever the family gathers for any kind of get-together. She has surprising stamina, especially when it comes to children and their high-energy lifestyle. My dad is home with the Lord now, but he equally enjoyed our family gatherings. He was amazed at God's kindness to us all and was quick to give Him credit for anything good that happened with us. In fact, he asked that his favorite verse in this regard be put on his tombstone: "But God..." (Eph. 2:4). And like him, I now look at the absolute grace of God upon us as a family and give thanks. I wish I could say this grace has enabled us to avoid problems, crises, and failure. It hasn't. But in the midst of it all, there remains grace. Great grace.

## THE RESPONSIBILITY OF FAVOR

I have so many people around me who are first-generation believers. They would do anything to have the momentum of grace in their family line as we do in ours. And while it is impossible to go back multiple generations and reset the direction of their family, it is possible through honor and humility to inherit this momentum of grace from a family who has this testimony.

Self-pity won't fix it. Accusing God won't help change the family line. But recognizing God's grace that rests upon another person is a big first step. In that place, we are more prone to give honor where it's due, which is obviously to our loving Father. He doesn't display favor on one person to create an awareness of lack in another. He does so to draw us to Himself that we might more fully apprehend what He has given to us through His Word. From there we can learn to honor what God has done and learn from their example.

I think it's even appropriate to receive prayer from them that God would impart to our family the grace that is on another's. God is able to impact an entire family line through such a prayer, so that they can live as though they too had multiple generations of believers. Only God can do this. But He can and will.

---

Anyone who has an increased measure of favor in an area of life is to live knowing it is a gift from God. It doesn't matter how hard I worked, how much I sacrificed, or how much I obeyed God. The end result is entirely a gift of God's grace. *#bornforsignificance*

---

Beni and I have done this when we recognized God's favor on people's lives in areas where we seemed to have little favor or breakthrough, and our lives were dramatically changed as a result. The point is, none of us need to lack. Ever. There is grace enough for us all to reign in every part of life. But we must embrace the process of humility and with thankfulness learn from one another. Because we are family and because we are individually members of one body, a breakthrough for one is to be a breakthrough for all.

Anyone who has an increased measure of favor in an area of life is to live knowing it is a gift from God. It doesn't matter how hard I worked, how much I sacrificed, or how much I obeyed God. The end result is entirely a gift of God's grace. When we realize this, it is much easier to give away the insights, experiences, and hopeful encouragement for others to benefit in the same way we benefited from the successes of others.

## OWN IT!

There are many who seem to feel bad for having God's blessings and favor on their lives. I remember a pastor who picked me up in his brand-new car. It was beautiful. I could tell he enjoyed it but that he also felt the need to explain how he got it. It was a gift from his congregation. Of course, I celebrated with him, but I also felt bad for him that he felt blessing needed an explanation. Most of us live with a subconscious need to apologize for favor. It's sad. But until we have an adequate theology of blessing, we will probably continue to do this.

You really never have to apologize for, explain, or feel guilty for favor. If you do, you've limited how much God can entrust to you. We often feel the need for explanations because we, as the church, don't yet have a sound theology for blessing that doesn't undermine the gospel message of Jesus. Attempts have been made, but to my way of thinking they are mere attempts to legitimize materialism that have failed miserably. We now have another chance. It is essential that we get this figured out without celebrating materialism or legitimizing accusations, suspicions, and jealousies that accompany such journeys as in the past.

Favor on a person is always to draw people to God. Blessings are to be the calling card of God for the lost.

> And yet He did not leave Himself without witness, in that He did good and gave you rains from heaven and fruitful seasons, satisfying your hearts with food and gladness.
>
> —Acts 14:17

Blessings are to be a witness of God's heart for people. The favor of God on one person's life is there to make people hungry for more. Jealousy is a cheap counterfeit, and in the end it undermines the invitation of God for more. When blessings rest upon another person's life, they should drive us to God. They should drive us to His Word that we might learn how to appropriate His promises more fully into our lives.

God is no respecter of persons. He is the same yesterday,

today, and forever. That means I qualify. By faith, I inherit the promises of God for myself in a given situation.

## DAVID MODELED IT

That is what happened to David when he saw the blessings of God on Obed-Edom and his family. Obed-Edom was a Gittite from Gath, a city of the Philistines. He was most likely one of the many Philistine expatriates loyal to David. (See 2 Samuel 15:18–22; 18:2.) This would explain why David would place the ark of the covenant (where the presence of God dwelt) in the home of a foreigner following the death of Uzza.

---

Favor on a person is always to draw people to God. Blessings are to be the calling card of God for the lost. *#bornforsignificance*

---

Uzza had extended his hand to steady the ark, which God called irreverent. He died as a result. Because of this loss, David was angry and afraid. I think it's safe to say David was now afraid of God Himself. For this reason, he put the ark in Obed-Edom's home instead of pressing on to bring the presence into Jerusalem.

But something happened. Blessing upon blessing began to flow into Obed-Edom's home. David heard about the favor that was resting on this family and decided the blessing was worth the risk. Therefore, he pursued God once again and attempted to bring the ark to Jerusalem. This time he followed God's Word more intentionally and succeeded as a result. It is unnatural not to pursue blessings when we see they are available. A false sense of humility has killed that God-given desire for more.

Is it possible the death of Uzza caused David to rethink what

God was like, causing him to withdraw from seeking His face? It's possible and even understandable. But it was the blessing that recalibrated his thinking, giving him the courage to take risks again and contend for what God had promised him.

I'd like to suggest that this was a key moment in David's life and, ultimately, in Israel's history. He moved past offense, self-pity, and all the other stumbling blocks discovered on the way to fulfilled purpose. Through David, the presence of God was restored to its rightful place: Jerusalem. Israel became more fully what God intended as a nation: a people of His presence. The blessing of God upon Obed-Edom awakened a passion in David to pursue more of God, made available through testimony and promise.

## JOB KNEW

Job was an extremely blessed man, and everyone in his day knew it. Even God bragged on him, calling him a "blameless and upright man, fearing God and turning away from evil" (Job 1:8). He was blessed with status, wealth, family, and favor.

His children were raised in the blessing of the Lord. While we don't know of their spirituality, we do know they were raised in a godly environment, tasting of God's goodness through their dad's heart for God. But Job knew the effect of blessing on the soul of a person, so he took deliberate steps to keep them covered and protected.

> His sons used to go and hold a feast in the house of each one on his day, and they would send and invite their three sisters to eat and drink with them. When the days of feasting had completed their cycle, Job would send and consecrate them, rising up early in the morning and offering burnt offerings according to the number of them

> all; for Job said, "Perhaps my sons have sinned and cursed God in their hearts." Thus Job did continually.
>
> —Job 1:4–5

I find this to be amazing. There is no record of sin or misbehavior. But Job in his wisdom knew the potential effect of a blessed life if the heart is not kept in check through thankfulness and humility. So he offered sacrifices on their behalf, which amounts to intercessory-type prayer in our day. He did this just in case something might have entered their hearts while they were feasting. He was concerned about what they might have thought in moments of abundance.

---

What does it look like when God's favor is carried well? He is glorified, we are strengthened, and the people around us benefit. *#bornforsignificance*

---

In keeping with this same theme, Proverbs 30:8–9 admonishes: "Keep deception and lies far from me, give me neither poverty nor riches; feed me with the food that is my portion, *that I not be full and deny you* and say, 'Who is the Lord?'" I want to draw your attention to the phrase I put in italics. The ultimate book on wisdom recognizes the ability of some to have abundance and then lose their touch with the Lord. It's not automatic, thankfully.

God is a perfect Father who looks for the chances to pour blessings into the lives of His children. But He is also a Father who loves us and doesn't want to increase our blessing beyond what we have the heart and maturity to carry well. What does it look like when God's favor is carried well? He is glorified, we are strengthened, and the people around us benefit. Once again, it is the disciplined heart with humility and thankfulness that enables us to survive and thrive with the high cost of blessing.

I want to draw your attention, again, to what the apostle Paul meant when he said that he had learned how to abound and how to be in need. He then gave the secret, "I can do all things through Christ who strengthens me" (Phil. 4:13, NKJV). We instinctively know we need strength when we're experiencing pain and lack. But Paul also knew he needed the same measure of strength when he was in abundance. Such humility and dependency are key for living in blessing without ruining its purpose. God's favor is always to endear us to Him as the source as well as give us the honor of representing Him in whatever area the favor functions.

## IT'S RARELY ABOUT MONEY

The last thing I ever wanted to write about in this book is money. I'm not afraid of the topic at all. It's just that so many have such an emotional limp in their walk with Christ that it's hard to communicate well. There are so many "triggers" in our various spiritual cultures that reactions abound, unnecessarily so. Regardless, I want this one section about money to communicate my values.

Four things matter to me in regard to money and possessions. I'm sure we could all list dozens of things, yet I've reduced my priorities down to these four that have become the guiding standards for decades.

1. **Generosity**. The first priority of resources, whether it's money, possessions, insights, or whatever, is to be generous. Beni and I have never given as low as 20 percent of our income in our forty-six years of marriage. We plan our financial

life first around the privilege to give and then the rest of our needs.

2. **Contentment**. Not having to "keep up with the Joneses" is a huge part of financial success in the kingdom of God. Being satisfied with what God has provided in a particular season is important. That doesn't mean it's wrong to move or that a greater amount of resources is evil. It simply means I must find the place of joy in whatever condition I'm in.

3. **Investments**. Each household should look for multiple sources of income. It is biblical wisdom to make money work for us. This is one of the most basic laws of finances. Money can work for us. And over time, because of the wonder of compound interest, income is exponentially increased. Contentment makes this possible because our lives are not defined by what we own.

   As I mentioned in chapter 1, I tell our folks that if they don't long for more, they're selfish. How can we be surrounded by such great need but not want to do something about it? To prove we're spiritually alive, we must pray to receive more from what God has reserved for those who live by the wisdom He provided.

4. **Excellence in purchases**. This may not seem important to many, but I consider it to be a great way to illustrate the kingdom lifestyle. Excellence is one of the primary expressions of wisdom. And to apply excellence in our purchase of goods

illustrates His nature. In my opinion, buying the best that we have the resources for illustrates proper care and wisdom. That looks quite different for me now than it did forty years ago. But the principle was the same. Many times over the years I've tried to save money (as a good disciple) for the kingdom and bought something that was not as high-quality as I could have. I don't think God has ever honored that decision, as it seemed to backfire almost every time. It is vital that we live to honor God in all we do. He is not a God attracted to the inferior.

## THE EXCELLENCE OF PROMOTION

I love the way God honors the lifestyle of excellence. He does so with promotion. Excellence is one of the many ways wisdom is manifested, and God looks to promote that in the earth. Don't mistake perfectionism for excellence. Perfectionism is different from excellence in the same way that religion (form without power) is different from the kingdom of God (the ultimate reality of God's presence and power). Perfectionism is religion, and excellence is kingdom.

Proverbs once again brings such clarity to the issue of promotion and the temptation promotion brings.

> Do you see a man skilled in his work? He will stand before kings; he will not stand before obscure men. When you sit down to dine with a ruler, consider carefully what is before you, and put a knife to your throat if you are a man of great appetite.
>
> —Proverbs 22:29–23:2

As stated earlier in the book, excellence is a key to promotion. But this passage gives us the warning of what to watch for once promotion comes. Put a knife to your throat. That's a rather crude description of the importance of self-imposed restriction. The one who lives with excellence as a standard for their life and labor will experience promotion in ways that others will never receive.

It is both a warning and blessing that promotion will bring a person into a company of people whose wealth, fulfilled purpose, and status are greater than theirs. The warning of wisdom is, "Put a knife to your throat if you are a man of great appetite." Herein lies the role of discipline: as I recognize what favor exposes me to and my own personal bent toward outward gain, I use self-imposed restriction that chooses the privilege of influence over the possibility of personal gain. To put it plainly, I can have the influence that excellence makes possible, or I can trade it for my lust for personal gain. But I can't have both.

## THE THEOLOGY OF BLESSING

We love it when people seek first the kingdom of God. But we're not always as happy with them when "all things are added" (Matt. 6:33) into their lives. We love it when someone gives in secret. But we're not always as happy with them when God rewards them openly (Matt. 6:4). We love it when people humble themselves under the mighty hand of God. But we're not always as happy with them when God exalts them in due time (1 Pet. 5:6).

---

I can have the influence that excellence makes possible, or I can trade it for my lust for personal gain. But I can't have both. *#bornforsignificance*

---

Each of these situations gives us the opportunity to grow into a kingdom mindset that rejoices in the promotion of another, or it gives us a chance to move in jealousy, which is often empowered through what is falsely called discernment.

Throughout history, there have been great moves of God that came to an abrupt end because of jealousy and competition. Yet it was never in the heart of God to end the increase of what He was doing in the earth. But in order to save those who were carrying that weight of glory, so as not to bless them beyond their capacity to bear, He withdrew the anointing.

We are at a place and time where I feel like the Lord once again wants to see what we can carry before Him responsibly. Will we be misunderstood? Of course. As I said earlier, Jesus was perfect, and He was misunderstood. I can't expect anything less. And while I never have to enjoy it, I do have the privilege of giving thanks in the middle of it.

I believe that the Lord would love to demonstrate His resurrection power. He'd love to demonstrate what it looks like to have a people who are finally out of the wilderness.

Israel went for forty years around the same mountain because they just couldn't learn the lesson of abandonment and trust. Today some people have gone without for their entire lives, and all the Lord is trying to do is teach trust, because once the trust issue is settled, you can be entrusted with a promised land.

To embrace the assignment that has been given to us—which is to disciple nations—we have to have this lesson down. I have to be OK with you getting the car I was praying for. I have to know how to celebrate *your* promotion when I was hoping it would be my turn.

---

Jesus was perfect, and He was misunderstood. I can't expect anything less. *#bornforsignificance*

---

Both Jesus and Solomon taught the same concept about stewarding another person's possession or experience. Here is Jesus' comment, "And if you have not been faithful in the use of that which is another's, who will give you that which is your own?" (Luke 16:12). Another person's possession, be it the promotion I wanted or the breakthrough I needed, is an opportunity to celebrate their promotion as preparation for my own. And the inability to celebrate somebody else's breakthrough as though it were mine actually pushes back my own experience of breakthrough.

In Weaverville, one of our key guys in the church was an accountant. He had an accounting office and did taxes and other services for businesses and so on. One of his competitors had just opened a brand-new office, and he was invited to come to the grand opening. He stayed for the whole party until everyone had gone home. He then explained that things were tight financially, and he was unable to bring a gift. But he asked if it would be OK to pray for God's blessing on the man. He said sure. So he prayed. He gave thanks for him and celebrated the goodness of God for prospering him. He prayed for increased blessing. By the time he was through, the "competitor" had tears in his eyes because he realized, "This is how His world works. In *His* world, it's possible for both businesses to succeed."

If you see somebody get a breakthrough that you were praying for, even if you have to force yourself, celebrate it. If you are jealous, sometimes giving a gift of honor will silence jealousy. Put something into action. Skip a meal and pray for them. Do something. It is vital that we starve jealousy to death by not giving it any attention.

## BEHIND THE SCENES

Some of those who are blessed outwardly in multiple areas of their lives are actually those who have paid a great price in seeking His kingdom (lordship) in every area of their lives. This moved God's heart for them in outward ways. In other words, these individuals are rewarded openly (visible to all) because of what they did in secret (invisible to all). This is done by our loving Father.

Oftentimes the one who seems to have it made financially is actually one who has been a secret giver to the things that God values. When God rewards openly, it brings that person's life into blessing but also scrutiny. Jesus said He would return a hundred times as much of what was given, with persecutions. (See Mark 10:30.) It's tragic that often the persecution comes from well-meaning believers.

When people are exalted or promoted to high places of influence, the average believer wonders what compromise they committed to reach that place. As I write this, a famous musician is boldly professing Christ, and much of the church is questioning his conversion. Jealousy is ugly and costly.

---

Celebrating another person's victory is often a key to our own. *#bornforsignificance*

---

The absence of a theology of blessing creates a vacuum that attracts deception and lies. It's weird, but this way of thinking often functions out of misapplied truth. In other words, a person feels justified in their opposition to one believer's wealth because they have a genuine hatred for materialism. When we reject a person over truth, it is usually misapplied, and we are functioning out of suspicion and not actual discernment.

It is time to settle some of these issues that have kept us from the place of influence for the kingdom of God and learn to celebrate another person's promotion without faltering through jealousy and accusation. Celebrating another person's victory is often a key to our own.

## BACK TO THANKSGIVING

I had an interesting experience in the middle of the night about three months ago. The Lord spoke to me that the key to mental health is giving thanks in everything, and the key to emotional health is always rejoicing. That approach to life is central to who God made us to be.

I am so thankful for the blessing of God upon my family and upon Bethel in general. Our gathering times are reminders that in spite of all our blemishes we live under the favor of God. The blessed life hasn't kept us from crises or failure. But we work hard to use that favor to serve people well and improve their lives through example, teaching, and personal relationships.

I also refuse to feel guilty for favor and blessing. Being apologetic for God's touch upon my life in order to prove to others that "I am not worthy" is another unhealthy position that is a complete waste of time. Such a posture appeals to people, as it masquerades as humility. But I don't believe it appeals to God. I would never want my children to apologize to their friends for how much I love them. Instead, my heart is that my love would release them to dream and celebrate life in ways otherwise kept out of reach.

Favor is a gift. If it were earned, it would be called wages, which means we could take credit for it. But it's not. Instead, we have the responsibility to use it for its intended purpose of glorifying God and causing others to benefit. Interestingly, using favor in this way causes it to increase.

I have learned that blessings can make one feel entitled and deserving instead of thankful and dependent. I don't want to make anyone paranoid, but after such a wonderful Thanksgiving holiday with family and friends, I felt the need to get alone with God. I did so with one thing in mind: I wanted my heart to be recalibrated anywhere it needed to be under the absolute lordship of Jesus over my thoughts, intentions, and actions. I wanted to be intentional about reaffirming my complete dependence on His grace. It's not that I had wandered in any way. In fact, even after my time in His glorious presence, He never addressed any inappropriate conduct, thought, or attitude that I needed to confess.

---

Favor is a gift. If it were earned, it would be called wages, which means we could take credit for it. But it's not. *#bornforsignificance*

---

Our family members had a wonderful time together. We celebrated with good food, enjoyed one another, and shared the wonderful stories of our lives as believers. It was all good. But I can feel the pull in times of abundance (family, food, and time to rest) to turn my attention to seek first "all these things" instead of seeking first the kingdom. It wasn't a feeling of guilt due to blessing. I believe it was wisdom, doing for myself what Job did for his own children.

## THE LIFE OF BLESSING

We must remember that while the new covenant is greater than the old covenant, and the blessings of the old should never surpass those of the new, herein lies a blessing that I believe made it through the cross unchanged. Aaron was given this decree to announce over God's people.

> The LORD bless you, and keep you; the LORD make His face shine on you, and be gracious to you; the LORD lift up His countenance on you, and give you peace. So they shall invoke My name on the sons of Israel, and I then will bless them.
>
> —NUMBERS 6:24–27

We have been predestined to live with the blessings of the Lord on our lives as calling cards that others would accept His invitation to receive His grace. While blessing is relative, according to our assignment in life, it carries the revelation of God's heart as a Father for all to receive. Learning to carry this may well be a key in seeing the kingdoms of this world become the kingdom of our Lord and Christ.

Comparing ourselves to others can lead only to wrong thinking and ultimately wrongdoing. It is the breeding ground for jealousy.

The theology of blessing is not to give us fat bank accounts. It's not to illustrate our greatness or giftedness. And it is certainly not to say we are better than someone else. What has been missing must be embraced to illustrate the success of the cross and its corresponding resurrection, to bring the ultimate illustration of a life well lived and the corresponding transformation to nations of the world. We have the distinct honor of demonstrating the effect of grace on our lives.

> Love has been perfected among us in this: that we may have boldness in the day of judgment; because *as He is, so are we in this world.*
>
> —1 John 4:17, nkjv

Lets' go back to one of the most remarkable statements in the whole New Testament. *As He is, so are we in the world*. It doesn't say as He was. Sometimes our concerns for excess cause us to miss truth. What is meant here? Does this mean we'll never need correction, repentance, growth, or discipline again? Of course not. This passage simply describes what we're being conformed into: the image of our victorious and glorified Savior! It's all about the glory of God upon His people.

---

Comparing ourselves to others can lead only to wrong thinking and ultimately wrongdoing. It is the breeding ground for jealousy. *#bornforsignificance*

---

Our lives are not patterned after the Christ headed to the cross. Yes, the life of the cross is still essential for us all. But it leads to something: resurrection. We are being conformed into the image of the One who is raised from the dead, ascended to the right hand of the Father, and glorified. We model the life of resurrection through victory. And sometimes we model the life endurance until the victory comes.

Picture a potter looking to a model and shaping the clay accordingly. We are being shaped by the Holy Spirit into the likeness of the model—Jesus Christ, the ascended One. He is glorified and at the right hand of the Father. All the egocentric, materialistic efforts to represent godliness through fleshly manifestations are counterfeit copies—and poor copies at that. We have the unique privilege of living the resurrection life here on earth as a demonstration of who He is for all humankind. God has designed all of us to become "one mature man—the fullness of Christ." This is His heart, His plan, and within His capacity to accomplish. May it happen in our lifetime.

> ...till we all come to the unity of the faith and of the knowledge of the Son of God, to *a perfect man*, to the measure of the stature of *the fullness of Christ*.
>
> —Ephesians 4:13, NKJV

We must give ourselves to learn how to live victoriously, reigning in life, "for as He is, so are we in this world" (1 John 4:17). It's time for that reality to be the living testimony of the church in this hour. This is all for His glory, for our strength, and for salvation to come to the nations. We were born *for such a time as this*, a time of increasingly great significance.

# NOTES

**Chapter 13**

1. "John Adams Quotes," Goodreads, accessed April 20, 2020, https://www.goodreads.com/quotes/42294-the-science-of-government-it-is-my-duty-to-study.

2. For more information on Hauge, I recommend reading *Revival and Society: An Examination of the Haugian Revival and Its Influence on Norwegian Society* in the 19th Century by Alv Johan Magnus, magister thesis in sociology at the University of Oslo, 1978.